Repairing the Apostolic Church

Rev. Nathaniel Morales & Rev. William H. Carey

Cover photo by Paul Winter

Ruins of St. Martin's Church

Wharram Percy,

North Yorkshire, England

1961

Used by permission

Dedication

This work is dedicated first and foremost to our Lord Jesus, for His great love and mercy. It is further dedicated to the men and women of God who labor to restore the original Apostolic church in all its power and truth. May your labors always be blessed with abundant harvest.

Where do you start when you have had so many wonderful teachers and men and women of God to thank for a lifetime of mentoring and discipleship? It is not an easy task. Someone once said that there is nothing new under the sun. While that may be true, we find that too many "new" things have crept into the body of Christ, and not enough things of true value and worth have been retained.

We count ourselves blessed to have been trained by men who knew only one source of truth – the Bible. There are many voices speaking in the world today, with opinions beyond counting. Yet the church of Jesus seems to be falling short of the glory and prominence it should be displaying to the whole Earth. We want us to be that city on a hill, the source of joy and blessing to all mankind. We can only be that when we operate and function as God designed us to do.

We had the wonderful opportunity to be trained for ministry by people of character, people who knew God. They instilled in us a love for the word of God and for the ways of God. We owe a great debt of love to those men and women. Some have already gone on to their reward, while others are still here fighting the good fight of faith.

Nathaniel Morales and William H. Carey

Table of Contents

Foreword

It would probably be wise to set in place some foundational thinking before we begin. The challenge is to set aside all preconceived ideas about what is meant by the words *Apostolic* and *Ministry*. Both of these words are used fairly liberally by the mainstay of churches, ministries and denominations on the Christian landscape today. Unfortunately, in most cases these words, concepts and ideas have been stripped of their biblical authority and power and have become just more victims to the devaluation of biblical truth.

Put simply, truth is not a list of dos and don'ts, and being Apostolic is much more than just doctrine. Being Apostolic is first and foremost the understanding that truth is a person – The Lord Jesus Christ.

It is interesting to read John chapter 5, and find the Lord speaking to a group of trained and revered religious leaders, and how He completely invalidates their scholastic and literal approach to God:

You search the Scriptures because you think they give you eternal life. But the Scriptures point to me! Yet you refuse to come to me to receive this life. John 5:39-40 (NLT)

How many churches and religious people use the scriptures to condone their own beliefs and to condemn and accuse others? Yet they miss the whole point: The scriptures were given as a way to point us to truth, not to become the embodiment of that truth. It's like that old saying "you can't see the forest for the trees." Life can only come from an encounter with, and surrender to, the Author of Life, and that will never be experienced by doctrines, formats, principles or interpretations of scripture.

There are thousands of young people who have left the traditional churches because they were never introduced to God. They were instructed. They were indoctrinated and they were dictated to, but they never experienced the Person who is the way, the truth and the Life!

So, what is Apostolic?

Apostolic is an understanding that God has finally and completely revealed Himself to all mankind through His incarnation as Jesus Christ.

He has revealed to all a way of life, love and forgiveness that leads to a right relationship with Him and with each other.

In the past God spoke to our ancestors through the prophets at many times and in various ways, but in these last days he has spoken to us by his Son, whom he appointed heir of all things, and through whom also he made the universe. The Son is the radiance of God's glory and the exact representation of his being, sustaining all things by his powerful word. Hebrews 1:1-3

God is no longer speaking to man only through the printed word or through the spoken media, but He came Himself and showed us that He is a God of Love and acceptance, and that He wants to have an ongoing relationship and intimate friendship with each and every one of us.

The bible is a telling of that story. It is a snapshot of how He lived and died and what He accomplished for us on the cross and through His burial and resurrection. The Bible is a personal invitation from the Creator of the universe to come and get to know Him.

Being Apostolic means never losing sight of what the story of the New Testament is all about. It means understanding that the power of that story and its effect on us today is just as life-changing for us as it was for the apostles who lived and walked with Jesus.

Being Apostolic is not just about believing in the infallibility of the Bible, but it's about knowing and personally experiencing the infallible God. Being Apostolic is about loving Jesus and treasuring His words and having Him speak to us on a daily basis.

Being Apostolic is not simply about preserving sound doctrine and holding to biblical truth. It's about awakening to the joy and wonder that the same Jesus the apostles knew and loved and served is the same Jesus we are so crazy about and walk with and worship today.

Acts 2:42 describes how the early Christians lived: They spent their time learning from the apostles, and they were like family to each other. They also broke bread and prayed together. When we today enjoy these same truths we are being Apostolic!

Being Apostolic is about living the message and the example of Jesus. The New Testament is a compilation of first-hand reports of His life, teachings, death, and resurrection. They were written down so that we would know His story from generation to generation. The bible is a love story, not a legal document.

Being Apostolic is understanding that God is looking for a family to enjoy, not religious adherents to control. It understands that His house has open doors and windows with no locks. Everyone is welcome and you can stay as long as you like. It's about love and forgiveness; it's about healing and restoration. It's about freedom and choice, not legalism and condemnation.

Today the word 'Apostolic' is used by many different churches to say that they trace themselves back to the apostles. For example, some 'orthodox' or traditional churches claim to be able to trace their leadership back to the apostle Peter, the so-called first 'pope,' and in this way consider themselves

But in our opinion, true Apostolic churches are those that love and accept people. They embrace the sinner where he is. They feed the hungry and clothe the naked. They take care of the widows and the orphans. They care about the sick and needy. Apostolic is not merely about a baptismal formula, but about a baptism of love.

Being Apostolic is about walking the walk, not just talking the talk. It's about the beatitudes and 1 Corinthians 13, the "love chapter." It's about holding up someone who has fallen, and being there when your neighbor comes calling.

What is Ministry?

We have seen many different styles of churches and ministries that run through the whole spectrum of human ideas and human inventiveness. Some were very effective in their particular place and time, and others were not very effective at all. We have seen tremendous variation in zeal and in abilities and in gifts of the Holy Ghost. We have also seen great tragedy and disgrace in ministry. So the question begs to be asked: Are the differences in the experiences and successes in the congregation directly related to the qualifications of the minister? Do weak ministers result in a weak congregation? We must ask if it is reasonable to judge and evaluate a minister by the spirituality and maturity of the congregation. What, really, is the effect of ministry on the congregation?

For years we have taught that the ministries of Ephesians 4:11 were for the equipping of the saints to prepare them to do the work of service (or ministry).

And He gave some {as} apostles, and some {as} prophets, and some {as} evangelists, and some {as} pastors and teachers, for the equipping of the saints for the work of service, to the building up of the body of Christ; until

we all attain to the unity of the faith, and of the knowledge of the Son of God,
to a mature man, to the measure of the stature which belongs to the fullness
of Christ. Ephesians 4:11-13 (NASB)

Then it would appear that the effectiveness of these five ministries should be seen in the growth of the saints into the work of service. If the saints continue to be just pew sitters, have the ministries failed to be effective? If the saints do not attain to the unity of the faith and to the full knowledge of the Son of God, have the five ministries failed? Is it necessary for the saints to get involved "in the ministry" in order to grow to this maturity? Let us suppose for a moment that the five ministries have equipped the saints to do the work of service, but the saints are too self-centered and selfish to step out and begin to minister.

Have the five ministries failed, or have the saints failed? Will the Lord still say to the five ministries, "Well done, good and faithful servant?" Will the Lord treat the five ministries as a unit and judge them as one or will each ministry be evaluated according to his own labor, even though there were no results in the saints?

Now, let us look at this from a different perspective: Suppose that our understanding of Ephesians. 4: 11 is clear, but our particular grace and calling is to be a pastor who teaches basic things. Will the saints ever come to the maturity to do the work of service or ministry and therefore grow by that involvement? Let us suppose also that there are no apostles, prophets, evangelists or teachers available to the local church. Is the pastor supposed to assume these roles? Are these four building ministries of apostles, prophets, evangelists and teachers itinerant – traveling ministries – or are they supposed to be raised up and active in each local church? Has "the church" placed too much responsibility on the "pastor," and then evaluated the pastor according to the growth and maturity of the saints? We could go on and on presenting an endless list of questions that are not answered clearly in scripture.

That there is a serious problem in the modern Apostolic church is undeniable. Because we have attempted to pattern our churches on the Protestant model, rather than the Apostolic model, we have seriously hindered church growth and effectiveness, as well as the efficacy of the five-fold ministry. One indication of this is the mega-church, where one pastor tries (unsuccessfully) to be all things to thousands of people, many of whom s/he doesn't even know. Another sign is when one city has anywhere from two to two dozen Apostolic churches of the same denomination. A third sign is idle ministers sitting on the platform of the church, not actively pursuing their calling.

In one U.S. city, there are two Apostolic churches less than half a block apart! Are they sharing the mission field, or competing with each other? While we can't control what another denomination does, we are able to make the right choices for ourselves. The chapters that follow teach the original Apostolic plan for church administration and growth. It is our hope and prayer that someday ALL Apostolic churches will see the wisdom of this plan, and abandon the man-made Protestant model currently in use.

One of the results of using the Protestant model of church administration (which in turn, is based somewhat on the Catholic model) is that certain commonly used terms no longer have the same meaning as they did in scripture. If we are going to follow the Apostolic model, then we need to abandon our current understanding in favor of the scriptural definitions. Here are some terms we will need to properly understand in order to proceed:

Apostle

Bishop

Pastor

Evangelist

Elder

Deacon

APOSTLE is a word that is largely misunderstood today. Some denominations designate their highest clergy as apostles, and such people do little other than administrate the church and make ruling policy. In other denominations, as well as some independent churches, we find pastors of large churches calling themselves Apostles. Some denominations avoid the term altogether, believing that there are no Apostles today. So we need to determine what an Apostle is, and if the office still exists today.

In Eph. 4:11-15, we see the exposition of the five-fold ministry, and the purpose of those five ministries in the church. If we carefully read verses 12-15, we can see that this goal has not been fully achieved, but is an ongoing process that will continue until the Lord returns for His church. Thus, logically, we must conclude that all five of the ministries mentioned in verse 11 are still in operation.

The word Apostle is derived from the Greek word ἀπόστολος (apostolos), which is created from a Greek verb that means "to send." An Apostle is one who is sent, like a delegate or an emissary. Specifically, an Apostle is one who is sent to a place where there is no church in order to begin a new work. This definition holds true whether the Apostle is sent to a local city or to a foreign nation. By this definition, it is clear that the office of an Apostle is identical to that of a missionary. So Apostles are not rulers, nor are they pastors of mega-churches. They are simply missionaries, those who go to a new city or nation to establish a church. Once the church is established, the Apostle ordains elders to take over the work (Titus 1:5), and then leaves to establish another work elsewhere, wherever the Holy Ghost leads.

BISHOP is a term that conjures up images of men in robes wearing miters and carrying shepherd's crooks. In some denominations, Bishops are overseers of several churches in several cities, and may be over literally hundreds of congregations. Sometimes, people called *Bishop* are simply pastors of large churches.

The Greek word translated as Bishop in the New Testament is ἐπίσκοπος (episkopos), and it derives from two words meaning *over* and *see*. In other words, a Bishop is an overseer, one who oversees the work of the church. In most modern usage, however, the field of a Bishop has been expanded far beyond what it should be. Each city is meant to have one Bishop, and for the first few hundred years of church history, it was so. But for one Bishop to oversee multiple cities or even entire states is not correct.

PASTOR is a word used by most denominations. In many places, a Pastor may lead a church that numbers in the thousands. The fact that it is impossible for one individual to provide that many with the necessary love, guidance, nurture, teaching, etc. required of a pastor is one of the reasons our churches are hurting so badly. We'll see further on that a Pastor was never meant to lead so many people.

The word Pastor is translated from the Greek word ποίμην (modern Greek pronunciation *peemeen*), which simply means *shepherd*. We know that in the natural, a shepherd is responsible to oversee a flock of sheep, to make sure they have sufficient food, water, shelter, protection from predators, guidance, etc. It is this personal, hands-on type of service that a Pastor provides for the church, but in a spiritual sense. The Pastor feeds the congregation with the word of God, protects them from wolves (in the spiritual sense) and from false teachings, offers spiritual guidance, etc.

EVANGELIST, which derives from two Greek words meaning Good News, is a preacher. Modern understanding is that the Evangelist is itinerant, that is, s/he travels around from city to city preaching. But a careful reading of Eph. 4:11 suggests this is not the case. The five ministries here were placed into the church for the purpose of equipping the saints. In other words, each church needs these five. Of the five, only one does not remain with the church. The Apostle, who founds the church, stays only until it is established and Elders have been ordained. But the Evangelist, the Pastor, the Prophet and the Teacher... these ministries remain. In the modern church, we try to force the Pastor to do all the work, from oversight, to teaching, to preaching, etc. No wonder so many burn out!

ELDER derives from the Greek word πρεσβήτερος (modern pronunciation *presveeteros*), which means a *senior*, or an *elder*. Although the Greek word can be used in the physical sense, that is, an older person, it has the figurative meaning of being leaders. Rather than being an office separate from Bishop or Pastor or Apostle, etc., Elder is a term that comprises all of those. Thus, an elder is any minister who is in a position of leadership.

"Let the elders who rule well be considered worthy of double honor, especially those who work hard at preaching and teaching." 1 Timothy 5:17 (NASB)

It is clear from this scripture that some elders did not preach or teach but they were still part of the ministry team in that city and worthy of that recognition and honor.

DEACON is a word that is somewhat underused in the church world today. Many positions in the church that should be understood as Deacons are not. Further, in some churches, Deacons are assigned tasks that are not really the work of a Deacon, such as baptizing and preaching. (While we can see from scripture that Deacons sometimes did go beyond that office and became preachers, evangelists, etc., such as Stephen and Philip, that work was not part of the office of a Deacon.)

The word Deacon is derived from the Greek word διάκονος (dhee-akonos) which refers to a person who runs errands, waits tables, performs ordinary tasks, etc. The Deaconate is a ministry of helps (1 Cor. 12:28). The Deacons do the work of running the church so that the Elders are free to attend to the word of God, to prayer, to preaching, etc. Some examples of Deacons in the modern church will be given in a later chapter.

The Bishop

And God hath set some in the church, first apostles,

secondarily prophets, thirdly teachers, after that miracles, then gifts of healings, helps, governments, diversities of tongues. (1 Corinthians 12:28)

Let all things be done decently and in order. (1 Corinthians 14:40)

Obey them that have the rule over you, and submit yourselves: for they watch for your souls, as they that must give account, that they may do it with joy, and not with grief: for that is unprofitable for you. (Hebrews 13:17)

Being a Bishop is a full-time job. It is unfortunate that many Bishops must also seek secular employment due to small church size or failure of the saints to tithe. The fact that a Bishop must sometimes seek outside employment does not alter the fact that overseeing even a small city is full time work. If the church is able, the Bishop should be paid a fair salary. (More on that in a later chapter.)

When churches are very large, the work is too much for one man or woman. (When we are speaking of a church here, we are not speaking in the modern sense of a building and congregation, but the church of a city, regardless of the number of congregations.) There are safeguards, too often ignored, built into the Apostolic church, to prevent the Elders from becoming overburdened. (We'll address those safeguards in subsequent chapters.) If a church is very large, an assistant Bishop may be helpful, but this should be a temporary solution. If the Apostolic pattern for the church is followed, an assistant Bishop won't be necessary, because the church will have Pastors and Deacons to relieve the burden on the Bishop.

The Bishop must be accessible. If the Bishop does not have a secular job, s/he should set aside a regular time to be available at the church during the week. Even if s/he must work outside the church, some effort should still be made to be available. Remember, Bishop: Your secular job may be your source of income, but the ministry is your calling. It is your true job, and infinitely more important than any other work. Don't ever lose sight of that truth!

Especially in larger churches, Bishops cannot possibly handle every problem, trauma and crisis in the lives of the Saints. And we all know that there are some folks who thrive on chaos, who will actually cause problems and then try to involve the ministry. The church has Pastors, and all such problems should be brought to them. Only if the Pastor is unable to deal with a problem should it be brought to the Bishop. (Of course, in a genuine emergency, if the Pastor is unavailable, the Bishop should be called. If the Pastor is available, s/he should make the decision of whether or not the Bishop needs to be notified.) It would be quite impossible for the Bishop to pray, read the Word, attend to the things of God, feed the flock, plan the services, etc., if every minor difficulty in the church were brought to his/her office.

Now please don't misunderstand: It's not that the Bishop doesn't care about people's troubles. On the contrary, if s/he doesn't care, s/he isn't called to be a Bishop! But just as Jesus, who also cares, entrusts this work to the Bishop, so, too, will the Bishop entrust parts of it to Pastors, people who are trustworthy and led by the Spirit. A Bishop who cannot delegate responsibility to others will burn out in a very short period of time.

The Pastor

Let us look again at the modern understanding of the Pastor, and contrast it to the biblical teaching. What really is the work of the pastor anyway? Is "pastor" a job description, a title, or a position in a local assembly?

Only in Ephesians 4:11 do we find the word "pastor," and that does not describe his/her work or function or position in the church. How then, can we evaluate a "pastor" and his/her effectiveness?

But wait! There's more - let us add to the confusion by looking at another scripture:

And God has appointed in the church, first apostles, second prophets, third teachers, then miracles, then gifts of healings, helps, administrations, various kinds of tongues. 1 Corinthians 12:28 (NASB)

This scripture does not seem to point to the universal church at large but rather specifically to a local assembly. However, again there is no mention of pastors here in this reference. No mention of elders appears either. Does this mean that pastors are only part of the universal church and have a limited function in the local assembly?

Since these things are not crystal clear we wonder why the local church has placed so much emphasis and responsibility upon one man or woman they call "pastor".

In most denominational settings "pastors" are transferred from one place to another when they are thought to be ineffective in a certain location. The denominational hierarchy and leadership would evaluate the pastors, and transfer those who are ineffective.

Because we have no specific scriptural criteria upon which to measure performance, it is very difficult to evaluate a pastor. If a person is ineffective in one ministry location, how do we know s/he will do better in another location?

Some say that "teachers" in 1 Corinthians 12:28 are synonymous with "pastors" in Ephesians 4:11. If this were true, either pastors or teachers would be redundant in Eph. 4:11, since both are mentioned as unique gifts and ministries.

Are "pastors" then a traveling ministry rather than a local ministry? What really is a pastor? No one seems to know, so every group makes up their own job description, and evaluates the pastor accordingly. However, we must come to the biblical and Apostolic understanding to know if "pastor" is a person, a title, a position, or a work that is accomplished by one person alone or by a team of people. If Christ has given "some pastors" as His gift to the church so that the church can come to maturity, then we need to know what this gift is!

Since we know so little about what a pastor is, how is it that we make "the pastor" the administrator, preacher, teacher, miracle worker, counselor and C.E.O. of this institution we call "the church"? This may be why "the pastor" is many times ineffective, because s/he is expected to be a jack-of-all-trades, but unfortunately, in most cases, s/he ends up being the master of none.

It is quite possible for a pastor to have God-given grace and patience to look after sheep, but have no ability, grace or anointing to preach or teach. (We have seen this many times) Does this mean that person is not called to be a pastor?

Let's pursue this line of thought: Let us suppose that a local assembly had four pastors. One had the grace to preach. Another had the grace to teach. Another had the grace to administrate. Another had the grace to shepherd the flock of God. Each person's grace would be used according to his/her own calling. Let us also suppose that the pastor who had abundant grace to shepherd the flock had no ability to administrate or to preach or teach and had no discernible spiritual gifts. Would s/he still be effective as a pastor? Yes! In conjunction with the others, therewould be one effective pastoral team.

Then why doesn't the church do this? Because we have developed a concept of the super-pastor who can do everything single-handed. However, God has not designed His spiritual body to function that way. We are all members of that body and we each have our unique place and function within that body. Each member is gifted and anointed to operate well in one function. Look at our own human body as a source of comparison. We do not see a "super member or special body part" that can do every other member's work. What we do see is a member who is a specialist in one function. The liver does not do what the heart can do. The lungs cannot do what the kidneys can do. Each "member" has its own purpose, design and function.

Is then a "one function pastor" to be considered poorly and judged as a failure because s/he is only effective in one area of ministry? No! The church should be taught to identify those who have abilities that "s/he" lacks and move them into those areas of ministry. Then the ineffective "pastor" suddenly becomes effective. The "pastor" who was messing up in areas that were outside of his/her grace, calling and anointing, and living in condemnation both from self and from others, becomes a success story. S/he has finally found the joy and purpose of being part of "the body".

Now if "pastor" is a title, a position, an authority, "the management", then s/he must wear all those hats because everything is his/her responsibility. If the pastor breaks down because of a misapplication or misuse of his/her gifts and calling, then in denominational circles that pastor is transferred to a different church or location where perhaps there will not be such great demands upon them. The "normal" thinking in these matters is that perhaps s/he will be able to get some rest and recover, and then get back to his/her responsibilities as "the pastor". If not, the usual course of action is a "strong" recommendation that s/he seek other (secular) employment where s/he will only be required to work eight hours.

The truth of the matter is, s/he actually broke down because s/he assumed, as do most churches and most Christians, that everything in the ministry of the church was the pastor's responsibility. But this is a concept that is foreign to the teachings of the New Testament. In plain words, there is no scriptural evidence to back up that assumption.

Let's look again at the scripture referring to the ministry gifts:

And He gave some as apostles, and some as prophets, and some as evangelists, and some as pastors and teachers, for the equipping of the saints for the work of service, to the building up of the body of Christ; until we all attain to the unity of the faith, and of the knowledge of the Son of God, to a mature man, to the measure of the stature which belongs to the fullness of Christ. Ephesians 4:11-13 (NASB)

We can see very clearly here that "pastors" (plural) is listed in a group of ministry gifts whose purpose is to work and function together to the end of building up the body of Christ. Pastors are in essence "a work" that is shared with several other gifted people. When this pattern is followed and allowed to flourish in the church, there is no reason for any one individual to experience burn out, or to break down due to overwork or overload.

If each ministry gift is allowed freedom and expression, and people are allowed to function according to each individual's grace, calling and anointing, the church as a whole is ministered to. The body of Christ is edified and built up. Certain ministry gifts can rest while others are functioning according to their own gift and anointing. Thus, there is little chance for fatigue and burn-out.

The modern understanding of the "pastor" is a relatively new concept, one that was not practiced as such in the Apostolic model. This modern understanding demands that the pastor oversee everything and control everyone else in "his/her" staff, and usually requires him/her to put his/her expertise into every function. This is not the principle of "body," and will, time after time, lead to "pastoral" burn out.

The average church today assumes that the pastor is supposed to do everything. If that were the case, however, then what would be the purpose and/or function of the apostle, the prophet, the evangelist and the teacher? Why does scripture name them as essential ministries, if the responsibilities were all to end up on the shoulders of one individual?

In some churches, it is "understood" that the pastor is the one who will minister in the spiritual gifts. For example, the pastor will usually be the one to give any messages in tongues and interpretations thereof. The pastor prays for the sick, and all things spiritual are his/her domain. This understanding is not scriptural, but has been accepted through ignorance and tradition. The Bible makes it clear that we are a "body," and that there are pluralities of ministry gifts to build up and edify the body. Yet, we have failed to operate as a body. Because of our lack of understanding, the pastor assumes all responsibilities for the ministry in the local assembly, and sooner or later burns out.

We have clear scriptural doctrine about the five ministries in Ephesians 4: 11, and then we also have the eight ministries that are listed in 1 Corinthians 12:28. Sadly, there has been little, if any, attempt to identify these ministries within the local assembly, or to allow them functionality within the confines of the current church mode. But the church cannot be managed and sustained and built up by one man's or woman's ministry alone. It is a biblical impossibility.

13

There are some pastors who ignorantly assume they possess all of these previously mentioned ministries within themselves. Many teach that they move from anointing to anointing as the need arises, and that the fullness of the ministry gifts abide in the pastor because s/he has been anointed of God to be in that position. It is dangerous to assume things that do not line up with scripture. Many practices are running rampant in the church simply because that is the way it has always been done. Unfortunately that is neither a solid nor a scripturally accurate position to take.

What we are in fact expressing and suggesting in our current church model is that the ministry of the pastor is the most important gift, and that the other ministry gifts are either not very important, or even unnecessary. Of course, sound biblical study reveals that this is not true.

All the ministry gifts are necessary and vital for the church to grow to maturity and to come to the full knowledge of the Son of God: The ministry of the apostle is important, but it is not the normal weekly ministry in the church. That Apostolic ministry gift may only be available once or twice a year to a local assembly. The ministry of the prophet is another that may not be a weekly occurrence in edifying the local church, but once it is recognized and in place, the local assembly can draw from that gift on a regular basis. Several times in scripture we see the prophetic ministry as a traveling ministry, being sent out at God's command and direction. However, we do see that in the church at Antioch there were prophets and teachers:

Now there were at Antioch, in the church that was there prophets and teachers: Barnabas, and Simeon who was called Niger, and Lucius of Cyrene, and Manaen who had been brought up with Herod the tetrarch, and Saul.

Acts 13:1 (NASB)

It appears that the function and work of the evangelist is focused upon the unsaved. While in modern practice, an evangelist is usually a traveling ministry, it should not exclusively be so. Evangelists are, by nature, preachers of Good News. Certainly, there is need to have the Good News preached in every local church. Teachers are required in every church. Without the ministry of teachers, people will not grow in maturity and understanding of the word of God, and will be easy targets for those carrying false doctrines. Clearly, all the ministries are necessary for the maturity of the saints, so they may do the work of service. While it is clear that the scriptures do not answer every question, it is equally clear that there are several ministries that should be working in the local church.

In recent years, there has been increasing interest in the recognition and implementation of the five-fold ministry gifts. There are books and seminars and even conferences on how to develop an Apostolic team or how to bring people into the "prophetic" ministry. While we may applaud the effort to unravel the ministry gifts and bring them back into open and unhindered use in the body of Christ, these attempts demand some scrutiny.

How do we test these ministries to know if they are valid? We might ask; how do you "teach" a person to become a prophet? It would seem that the person would first have to have a calling and a special grace from God, in addition to a special anointing from the Holy Ghost. In other words, are the ministry gifts imparted, or are they learned? The concern is whether the anointing of the Holy Ghost will flow from a ministry, or will it be just another human effort to try to produce Godly results?

Anything that does not come from the hand of God, regardless of the good intentions behind it, will ultimately produce death! Are we so dead to the truth of God that we believe that we can train or instruct an individual on how to become a pastor? Are the ministry gifts the result of human intellect and learning, or are they a divine impartation and calling from God? Whom God calls, God equips!

Christianity as a religion has approached the problem of needing a supply of pastors and ministries by establishing schools of ministry. Once you graduate and are properly credentialed, then you are automatically a "pastor". But the question is, did God really give this particular individual as a gift to the church, or did the individual "call" him/herself? Christianity as a religion, with good intentions, using its seminaries and religious schools, has contributed to the problem of counterfeit pastors, producing men and women who have no calling, discipline, grace or anointing. After having been "trained," they seem to think they can function in all the ministries as a one-man or one-woman leadership. The name "pastor" has taken on the meaning of C.E.O. Because of this, the church functions more like a corporation, with all operations reporting to and subject to the C.E.O., than like a body.

However, even if the church were supposed to operate as a corporation, no successful corporation would pick a C.E.O. the way we appoint pastors. The successful corporate president knows s/he has severe limitations, and therefore depends upon many others to make the day to day decisions that determine the successful turn out of a product.

In the secular corporate world, the boards of directors do not pick a man or woman to be president because s/he can do every job in the factory, but because s/he has the ability to form a team of leaders who know each job, and who, working together, can build a successful and profitable company. Jesus put it this way:

And the lord commended the unjust steward, because he had done wisely: for the children of this world are in their generation wiser than the children of light. Luke 16:8 (KJV)

We know the church is not a corporation in the worldly sense, but in practice it can be compared to that concept. The church is designed to produce a product. The product is mature Christians who function as a body and who have grown up in all things into Christ. The product must be up to the standard of Christ. There is only one C.E.O. in the church, and He is sitting on the throne of heaven. The president of our factory is the Holy Ghost. The various operational leaders and department heads are the apostles, prophets, evangelists, pastors and teachers, elders, deacons, administrators, miracles, healings, helps and various kinds of tongues.

All these operational leaders report to the Spirit for daily meetings. He adjusts the various operations to fit the needs of the finished product. The Holy Ghost must decide when to ship the product so it can be put into use. If it is still defective, He will not permit it to be shipped. The pastors have a definite work to do in producing the product, but they must stand **with** all the other operations leaders, and not in place of them. The pastor is not the president, but must report to the Spirit, like all the other department heads. "Pastors" who try to be presidents will eventually break down because they are out of their realm of grace and function. Humility and a spirit of teamwork are the basic building blocks and the best qualities any "minister" must have, regardless of the type of ministry operation or gift s/he has been called and anointed to function in. His/her life's work is to see change and growth in the people that God has brought into his/her sphere of influence. This is the lifestyle of Jesus Christ! And it necessitates total commitment and a mature character.

The ministry gifts should never be evaluated by the same standards as an hourly employee. Ministry is not an assembly line, and the ministry gifts are not factory type workers who must turn out so many good products a day that meet certain quality standards. A housekeeper may be evaluated by the cleanness and order of his/her home. A cook may be instantly evaluated by the food s/he prepares. But that is not how we determine value and purpose in the Apostolic ministry.

The New Testament gives us specific and detailed personal qualifications for elders and deacons but we have no standard upon which to measure their effectiveness in their work. A person who meets the personal requirements of an elder and deacon, as listed in scripture, may turn out to be a poor elder or deacon. This is true of any minister, including a pastor or a teacher. We may judge a prophet by waiting to see if what s/he prophesies comes true. In the meantime, a false prophet can do a lot of damage. Paul refers to the signs of an apostle, but he also speaks of false apostles. The teachers who came to Antioch from Jerusalem and taught the Gentiles that they must be circumcised obviously had met the basic standards of teachers, but their message was flawed.

Denominational leadership cannot closely monitor traveling ministries like Paul and Barnabas. Pastors, for the most part, are more or less left on their own today, and generally just answer to themselves. It is obvious that there is a lack of accountability in the current church system. This situation is immediately remedied when we return to the Apostolic pattern of a plurality of leadership in the local church. Where all the ministry gifts (plural) are functioning, there is built in accountability and control. The elders watch over the flock and over themselves. All work together to keep the church focused on the things of God, and to keep themselves within the boundaries of God's grace, blessing and individual calling. We may call it body discipline or community life-style, corporate anointing or spiritual accountability, but it must result in some internal manifestation that sets all the ministers on the right and stable track.

We must seek to return to the Apostolic pattern of New Testament ministry, as that is how things are supposed to be.

Ministers

We are using the term "minister" to represent all the various ministries in a local assembly. This will be helpful in discussing the challenges, the strengths and the weaknesses associated with "the ministry" or "leadership".

First, if a minister doesn't understand what the finished product is that s/he is working towards, s/he may have a tremendous ministry that is producing the wrong product. It would be like a president of a pharmaceutical company turning out an impressive amount of candy and chocolates and cookies, but producing no medicines. The minister may have a lot of training, education and impressive degrees in theology, but have no idea of what he is producing in the lives of the church. People may flock to hear him/her preach, but the message is having no effect in their lives.

Second, there is the issue of handling time. If the minister is controlled by activity, busyness and the constant flow of events each day, then the demands upon his/her time are out of control. The minister's time belongs first to God and the word, not to anyone who demands it. This misunderstanding of ministry priority produces pressure, ineffectiveness and lack of ministry performance. It kills the anointing.

Third, it is not unusual for a minister to be forced into ongoing functions or responsibilities in areas that have nothing to do with his/her calling. Some ministers are involved in sports programs, or recreation programs, or counseling, or just the maintenance problems of the building. It is all too easy for a minister to try to do everything, thus being sidetracked from his/her actual calling.

A true story illustrates this: A particular pastor called a friend of his who was an apostle. The pastor was discouraged and frustrated. He related how he had done so much, so many things, and yet his ministry did not grow and the church remained small. He asked his friend if he had any insight into what was wrong. The apostle could not argue with the fact that the pastor had done much and had worked very hard. He promised to seek the Lord for wisdom for the pastor's situation. That night, the Lord woke the apostle from a sound sleep and instructed him to turn on his computer and to begin to type. The Lord began to dictate a parable:

There was a man whom the Lord called, instructing him to climb a particular mountain. The mountain was extremely high and steep, and the peak was hidden in the clouds. The man was terrified, and refused to even try.

The Lord called a second man, instructing him to climb the same mountain. This man was also afraid, but he was obedient, and began to climb. For hours and hours, he climbed, sometimes just crawling. Hours turned into days, and his hands and feet were sore and bleeding, and his clothing was torn. He was exhausted, and finally, he gave up, and went back down.

The Lord called a third man, instructing him to climb the same mountain. Like the two before him, he was also afraid, but he was obedient, and began to climb. Like the man before him, he climbed for days, sore, tired, bleeding, with his clothes shredded from the rocks. And still, he pressed on. Finally, one day, totally exhausted, he looked up ahead, and he could see the top of the mountain! It was so near! And he began to climb again, but then, he collapsed from exhaustion, and died. He found himself standing before the throne of God. Immediately, he burst into tears, and fell to his knees with his face to the ground. "Oh, Lord," he cried, "I failed you!" "What do you mean? How did you fail Me?" the Lord asked. Looking up, the man replied, "I never reached the top!" Immediately, the Lord rose from His throne and rushed down to the man. He put His arms around him, held him, and said, "My dear child, you did not fail Me. I never asked you to reach the top. I only asked you to climb!"

The next morning, the apostle called the pastor to tell Him the parable. The answer to the pastor's question was in the parable. He was failing because he was trying to do all kinds of things that God had ever asked him to do. God had called him to perform a specific function, and he was trying to do that and everything else, too. The lesson for us is clear.

Fourth, since the minister feels responsible for the whole overall function and effectiveness of the church work, s/he is interested in the results. S/he spends too much time evaluating the objective work, instead of what God is saying within the church. The objective work of the church is the sum total of the function of **every** member, and generally cannot be measured. The effectiveness of each member and his/her output is directly related to the input and inspiration from within. In other words, what happens within reflects upon what happens without.

The effectiveness of the church can only be measured in how it changes its surrounding environment, and not in the depth of the message that is preached behind closed doors. If guidance, inspiration, vision and zeal is generated within the church, then there should an outward work by the members. Too often, however, the members are waiting for the "ministry" to do both the inside *and* the outside work. If the ministry buys into that idea, it soon loses its effectiveness inside. Of course, the work of the apostle and the evangelist may be focused outside in establishing churches, but the outward success of the church is established from the work within. The apostle doesn't stay in one location to become a "pastor". They do their work and move on. Then it is the new church's responsibility to preach and extend itself.

Speaking solely from the concepts presented in scripture, most ministers are actually specialists, and not general practitioners who handle all areas of ministry. When we come across a minister who claims to be able to do everything, we know s/he is operating in ignorance, pride or in the flesh. Bottom line, s/he is just running on pure human effort and human power. It is only a matter of time before s/he will run out of gas and break down. God has not designed the body so that one member can do everything. Each member has specific power, grace, calling and anointing to fulfill the function of his/her position in the body. An indifferent, lazy or comatose member has no place in the body of Christ.

Further, there is no such thing as an unnecessary member. Everyone has a purpose and a God-given ability, and the body will never mature into its place in God's eternal scheme of things until all of us come into an understanding of the body.

On the other end of things, there is little value in a member who doesn't need anyone else because s/he thinks s/he can do everything alone. Such a person will never produce lasting results, and will burn out and usually take others down, too.

These days, a search committee is organized to look for a new pastor (usually because the last one burned out). The most common mistake is to look for someone who can do everything him/herself. The reasoning behind this mindset is that since we pay him/her good money, s/he should do all the work. As a result, the pastor becomes a hireling instead of a gift of Christ to the church.

On a side note, search committees are not the biblical pattern for choosing a pastor. We tend to do things based on tradition and historical patterns, instead of relying on what the Bible teaches.

But if a search committee is formed, they should at least look for a specialist who not only does his/her thing well, but insists upon everybody else also doing their thing well. Churches that will only accept "the super minister" will end up being disappointed, unless they expect him/her to work mainly in the flesh.

That superbly gifted "super minister," the one who can do everything, will ultimately be found to be superbly incompetent. This isn't because s/he is not gifted or called of God, but because God has not designed the body to function that way. God is not going to give one person the anointing to do the work of other members, so they can then sit around and do nothing! When did being a disciple of Jesus Christ become a spectator sport? We think we can appoint one man or woman to lead the church and run all things spiritual, and that we only need to show up one day a week to be entertained! That may work for a Broadway production, but it does not work for the Church of the Living God!

It is important to realize that higher education and doctoral degrees are not necessarily an aid to effectiveness. Sometimes, they can actually accomplish the opposite. There are many studious, intelligent and intellectual ministers who, because of their preparation, now have no function within the body. Their great education and expertise in too many fields have set them above the body. They become judgmental, critical and abusive of the other members in the body, and can no longer function as members of the body, but instead, try to control it.

And God has appointed in the church..1 Cor. 12:28

The ministries are set IN the church... as a part of the body, not above the church, or as directors of the church. 1 Corinthians 12: 12-27 makes this abundantly clear. One error that has attacked the church from time to time is that the ministries are set in the head, and the "believers" are set in the body. However, in the church, Christ is the head, and all who are part of Him are set in the body. The ministries are members who are set in the body for a specific function. For "we" are one body, not "they" are one body. Contrary to popular opinion, the minister is not some universal guru who knows all and sees all. S/he sees through a dark glass like everyone else. However, hopefully, s/he will have a God given ability and anointing to do at least one thing effectively.

Ministry is hard work and the minister must control as much of his/her time as possible. Some ministers complain that they are so busy that they have no time to pray, read the bible, prepare a message, or fellowship with their family. In that case, we would have to wonder if they could possibly have an "effective" ministry. They are involved in much about nothing. This can only indicate that they think the whole burden of the church is upon them, that they are some kind of "super pastor." They are evidently trying to control everything, when they can't even control their time! It further indicates that they are ignoring the gifts and strengths of other members. If a minister cannot recognize his/her own weaknesses, s/he will surely not recognize his/her own strengths. And if s/he cannot recognize his/her own strengths, s/he will not recognize the strengths of the other members.

When you recognize your own weakness, you have to force yourself to set priorities for your time. If you see that God has designed an entire body to do the work, you will recognize the need for plurality of input and for the contribution of the other members of the body.

The minister must be honest and begin to set priorities by making certain determinations, such as "What is the grace and calling in my life? What is it that God expects of me"? The goal of any minister should be not to be so consumed with the "work" that needs to be done by him but rather to focus on what needs to be jointly accomplished by the whole leadership team for the edification of the local assembly.

We also need to adjust our thinking to the fact that "one body" does not mean that every member will have the same opinion as ours. Ten members may have ten opinions that differ from the opinion of the minister. This is when we need to recognize the strengths of different members. They may be experts in fields where we know very little. This is the wrong time to cancel out all their opinions by declaring, "God told me," "God anointed me," "This is my responsibility," or "God has set me in authority." Others' opinions may be God instructing you. We can waste so much time following our own wrong opinions. This is the biggest failure of the "one Pastor" mindset. Proper decisions can be made out of opposing opinions. Opposing opinions should not be treated as rebellion.

The seemingly great problem of having no available time can be solved by not spending time on things that contribute nothing to the work that you must accomplish. Most wasted time is spent on things that are irrelevant and contribute nothing. Time to pray, study, relax and think is not wasted time. Being busy doing things that are not part of your particular calling is a waste of time.

One Church Per City

And when he had considered the thing, he came to the house of Mary the mother of John, whose surname was Mark; where many were gathered together praying. (Acts 12:12)

And a certain woman named Lydia , a seller of purple, of the city of Thyatira, which worshipped God, heard us: whose heart the Lord opened, that she attended unto the things which were spoken of Paul. And when she was baptized, and her household, she besought us, saying, If ye have judged me to be faithful to the Lord, come into my house, and abide there. And she constrained us... And they went out of the prison, and entered into the house of Lydia: and when they had seen the brethren, they comforted them, and departed. (Acts 16:14-15, 40)

Greet Priscilla and Aquila my helpers in Christ Jesus: Who have for my life laid down their own necks: unto whom not only I give thanks, but also all the churches of the Gentiles. Likewise greet the church that is in their house. Salute my well-beloved Epaenetus, who is the firstfruits of Achaia unto Christ. (Romans 16:3-5)

The churches of Asia salute you. Aquila and Priscilla salute you much in the Lord, with the church that is in their house. (1 Cor. 16:19)

Salute the brethren which are in Laodicea, and Nymphas, and the church which is in his house. (Colossians 4:15)

And to our beloved Apphia, and Archippus our fellow-soldier, and to the church in thy house. (Philemon 2)

The first church did not have church buildings as we do. Since the first Christians were Jewish, they met on the Sabbath in synagogues or, in the case of the Jerusalem church, in the Temple. They also met in private homes during the week. It wasn't until after the Gentiles entered the church that buildings specifically for Christian worship were needed, since the Gentile Christians were not welcome in the Temple and synagogues. But when the Gentile church did build such structures, they did not abandon the Apostolic methods used by the Jewish Christians. They simply substituted their new buildings for the Temple and synagogues.

Over the centuries, the Apostolic methods were abandoned by people who misunderstood their purpose. For example, some believed that the first century church met in private homes simply because they had no place else to meet. But that wasn't the case at all. There were sufficient financial resources in the Apostolic church to build church buildings, and when the need arose, they did so. But home meetings were a vital part of both the Jewish and Gentile Christian churches.

The first century church was one Body, as the Apostolic church should be today. But geographical distance and ethnic (Jewish, Gentile) differences necessitated a type of division, even if it was in name only. Therefore, they began to refer to church groups by city names: "The church in Corinth," "The church in Jerusalem," etc. While we're on the subject of identifying local congregations, we need to look at a practice that existed in the first century church, and exists in a modified form now. But this isn't a good practice, and Paul rebuked those who followed it:

"Now this I say, that every one of you saith, 'I am of Paul;' 'and I of Apollos;' 'and I of Cephas;' 'and I of Christ.' Is Christ divided? Was Paul crucified for you? Or were ye baptized in the name of Paul?" (1 Cor. 1:12-13)

People in the early church were identifying themselves and others by the minister who had converted them. Paul correctly pointed out that he had not died for them, and they had not been baptized in his name. They did not belong to him or to Cephas (Peter), or any other minister. They, as is the case with all of the church, belonged to Jesus. Today, we have a tendency to identify congregations by the name of the pastor: "I go to Brother Smith's church." "They like to visit Sister Jones' church when they are in town." But if I may paraphrase Paul, was Brother Smith crucified for you? Or were you baptized in the name of Sister Jones? Of course not. Jesus was crucified for us, and we were baptized in Jesus' name. Thus, we, the entire church, belong to Jesus. Therefore, it is incorrect to identify a church as belonging to the pastor. The proper method of identifying a church is by city (the church in Las Vegas, the church in Indianapolis), or by more specific location (the church that meets in Sis. Miller's house, the church on Fourth Street). This may seem trivial, but it is the same situation Paul was addressing in 1 Cor. 1:12-13; and in 1 Cor. 3:4, he indicated that those who divided the church in that way, assigning "ownership" or affiliation by the name of a minister, were being carnal. Carnality is something we should flee. So please, let us remember Who was crucified for us, and in Whose name we were baptized. The church belongs to no one but Him.

In the first century, each city had one church. That is, there was one congregation that met weekly in one building, whether the Temple, the synagogue, or a Gentile church building. That congregation was comprised of small groups, small enough to meet comfortably in a private home. Priscilla and Aquila had a group in their home, Lydia had a group in hers, and Mary, the mother of John Mark, had a group in hers (Rom. 16:3-5; Acts 16:40; Acts 12:12). But the small group that could fit in a home wasn't the sum total of the church in that city. It was one group out of many in the city.

You'll find cities today with two or more Apostolic churches of the same denomination. This is wrong. The Apostolic pattern allows for only one church (again, we're talking about congregations here) and one Bishop per city. Let's visit a hypothetical first century city and its church. We'll work with a Gentile church, since most Christians today are Gentiles.

We'll call our hypothetical city "Poli" (Greek for *city*). The city of Poli has about 70,000 inhabitants.

The Bishop of the church at Poli is Brother Stephanos. Because the Saints of Poli are not Jewish, they are not welcome in the synagogue in the neighboring city. For this reason, Brother Stephanos and the Poli church built a large hall for their meetings. But it is used only one day a week. Why? Let's meet some of the Saints of Poli and find out.

Sister Phoebe is one of the Saints in Poli. She is called a Pastor. On Tuesday evening, twelve Saints gathered in Sister Phoebe's home in southeast Poli. They sang to the Lord and worshiped together. Then they shared with each other their prayer requests, praise reports, needs, etc. Then, as a group, they ministered to each other, according to their needs. Afterward, Sister Phoebe taught a lesson from the Bible. Then there was more praise and singing, followed by a time of informal fellowship. Brother Demetrios brought some cake, which they all shared. Sister Paula had brought her neighbor lady with her. This visitor was deeply impressed by the way the Saints ministered to each other. She asked for prayer for healing, and as the Saints laid hands on her, she was healed.

In other parts of the city, one hundred and forty-five other groups just like this one were meeting in the homes of Pastors. Over the next three nights, four hundred and thirty-five other groups met.

When the Sabbath[1] came, all the Saints from all the groups, with their Pastors, met at the church's meeting hall for worship service. Sister Vic-

---

1   Sabbath: Saturday. Whether the church meets on Saturday or Sunday is not important. The reason why Poli meets on the Sabbath will be explained later.

toria, an Evangelist, preached to them from the Word of God. The visitor from the group in Sister Phoebe's home also came to church and Sister Phoebe baptized her in Jesus' Name and she came up out of the water speaking in tongues. Twenty-five other visitors were also in church that day.

Monday nights there are no group meetings. Instead, Brother Stephanos meets with all the Elders at the meeting hall. They minister to each other according to the things the Spirit of God has been showing them, and they all pray for each other. Also present are future ministers, including future Pastors, the men and women who will lead new home groups. These meetings are part of their training for the work to which they are called. (More on how new groups form in a moment.)

It's important that we understand all this. The church at Poli numbers almost 7,000 people and is growing rapidly. It would be impossible for Brother Stephanos to minister to so many. But at the home meetings, they minister to each other's needs. The home groups are small enough that the Pastor can do what Brother Stephanos could not possibly do for the whole church. Visitors coming to the home groups can receive personal attention and their needs can be ministered to as well.

When a home group grows beyond an appropriate size, maybe fifteen people, it divides into two groups, each with its own Pastor. (For example, when the group in Sister Phoebe's home grows too large, it will divide in half. One half will continue to meet in Sister Phoebe's home, and she will continue to be their Pastor. The other half will no longer meet at Sister Phoebe's home, but will meet instead at the home of Brother Demetrios, who is to be their new Pastor.)

Now, the thought of division frightens some people. After all, we want to see the church grow, and division sounds counterproductive. But in nature, division is a common form of reproduction. Single-cell animals (amoebas, etc.) multiply by dividing! A home group of fifteen, dividing into two groups, can soon be two groups of fifteen, ready to divide into four.

This hypothetical pattern still works in the twenty-first century. The pattern is Apostolic, and all of the Apostolic churches should be using it.

The Deacons

And in those days, when the number of the disciples was multiplied, there arose a murmuring of the Grecians against the Hebrews, because their widows were neglected in the daily ministration. Then the twelve called the multitude of the disciples unto them, and said , It is not reason that we should leave the word of God, and serve tables. Wherefore , brethren, look ye out among you seven men of honest report, full of the Holy Ghost and wisdom, whom we may appoint over this business. But we will give ourselves continually to prayer , and to the ministry of the word. And the saying pleased the whole multitude: and they chose Stephen, a man full of faith and of the Holy Ghost, and Philip, and Prochorus, and Nicanor, and Timon, and Parmenas, and Nicolas, a proselyte of Antioch: Whom they set before the apostles: and when they had prayed, they laid their hands on them. And the word of God increased: and the number of the disciples multiplied in Jerusalem greatly; and a great company of the priests were obedient to the faith. And Stephen, full of faith and power, did great wonders and miracles among the people . Then there arose certain of the synagogue, which is called the synagogue of the Libertines, and Cyrenians, and Alexandrians, and of them of Cilicia and of Asia, disputing with Stephen. And they were not able to resist the wisdom and the spirit by which he spake. (Acts 6:1-10)

When they heard these things, they were cut to the heart, and they gnashed on him with their teeth. But he, being full of the Holy Ghost, looked up steadfastly into heaven, and saw the glory of God, and Jesus standing on the right hand of God, And said, Behold, I see the heavens opened, and the Son of man standing on the right hand of God. Then they cried out with a loud voice, and stopped their ears, and ran upon him with one accord, And cast him out of the city, and stoned him: and the witnesses laid down their clothes at a young man's feet, whose name was Saul. And they stoned Stephen, calling upon God, and saying, Lord Jesus, receive my spirit. And he kneeled down, and cried with a loud voice, Lord, lay not this sin to their charge. And when he had said this, he fell asleep. (Acts 7:54-60)

And God hath set some in the church, first apostles, secondarily prophets, thirdly teachers, after that miracles, then gifts of healings, helps, governments, diversities of tongues. (1 Corinthians 12:28)

Likewise must the deacons be grave, not double-tongued, not given to much wine, not greedy of filthy lucre; Holding the mystery of the faith in a pure conscience. And let these also first be proved; then let them use the office of a deacon, being found blameless. Even so must their wives be grave, not slanderers, sober, faithful in all things. Let the deacons be the husbands of one wife, ruling their children and their own houses well. For they that have used the office of a deacon well purchase to themselves a good degree, and great boldness in the faith which is in Christ Jesus. (1 Timothy 3:8-13)

The Saints of the church in Jerusalem sold all their possessions and put the money into a common treasury. From this treasury, the needs of all the Saints were administered. (Note that this was a *voluntary* system, freely chosen by the Saints in Jerusalem. There is no evidence that the other churches adopted this system, nor is it obligatory for churches today.)

One of the obligations placed upon all the churches, though, was the support of widows (specifics in a later chapter). In the Jerusalem church, the needs of the widows were taken care of from the common treasury. A problem, however, soon arose. It was alleged that the Grecian widows (Greek or *Hellenized* Jews) were being neglected in favor of Judean widows. The matter was brought before the Elders of the Jerusalem church.

As the ministers there correctly pointed out, it was not right that they should have to abandon the work of God to go wait on tables. The work of the ministry was too important, and they couldn't neglect it simply to oversee the distribution of food, etc. Although this problem was the only one of this nature reported, it brought to the forefront the fact that there is a tremendous amount of work involved in church administration, over and above the work of the Gospel. It is still not right for the ministry to neglect their calling in order to attend to such things.

This brings us to the solution: Deacons. In Jerusalem, seven young men were chosen to oversee the distribution of food, etc., to the widows. But that is just one facet of the work of a Deacon. The Deacons should be doing as much of the physical work involved in church administration as possible. The Deaconate is a ministry of service or "helps" (1 Cor. 12:28).

Today, most true Deacons are people with other titles. In point of fact, church secretaries and treasurers are Deacons. So is the person who mows the lawn, cleans the church, seats the visitors, etc. If a Deacon works full-time for the church, s/he should receive a salary for this work. There are requirements for the position of Deacon, as outlined in the scriptures at the beginning of this chapter. These requirements are important and should not be ignored.

Running a church office is quite a difficult job, and the larger the church grows, the more difficult this job can become. Any church that has more than a tiny handful of people needs at least one Deacon to do office work.

A church office needs at least one secretary, that is, a Deacon to run the office. There are phones to answer, letters to type and mail, incoming mail to sort, distribute, etc., filing, etc. Some correspondence will be letters dictated by the ministry, other will be "automatic" correspondence. Automatic correspondence is mail that goes out without specific authorization from the Bishop -- For example, every new visitor to the church should receive a letter of welcome within a day or two of his/her visit. In addition, if a Saint misses more than two services (without notifying the church that s/he wouldn't be there), some contact should be made, preferably a visit or phone call from the Pastor, but at least a letter from the church expressing concern and asking if assistance is needed. The secretary, or another Deacon, may also be responsible for putting together a church newsletter, for ordering or printing tracts, etc.

A church also needs a treasurer. This is a Deacon who is responsible to deposit the tithes and offerings of the Saints into the bank, and to disburse funds to meet all the church's expenses. Although the treasurer should handle as much of this as possible, s/he should submit a complete financial report to the Bishop at least once a month, preferably once a week. In addition, the church's checking account should be set up so that all checks need the Bishop's signature in addition to the treasurer's. Each week, or daily, depending upon the church's operating needs, the treasurer should submit checks to the Bishop for signing, along with a brief explanation of what each check is for.

Requests for funds from the various departments (Sunday School, Widow's Support, etc.) should be submitted to the treasurer, who may approve routine requests. For example, if the Sunday School usually operates on $150 a month, and asks for $160 this month, that's not an unusual request, and the treasurer may approve it. On the other hand, if the Sunday School asks for $500 to buy a new overhead projector, they should also submit a statement explaining their need, and the treasurer should get approval from the Bishop before writing a check.

Without Deacons, a church cannot function properly. The Elders of the church must be able and willing to delegate this work to those who are qualified, willing and able. Even today, no man or woman of God should be called away from prayer, study, preaching, teaching, etc., to go wait on tables, mow the lawn, shovel snow, paint the Sunday School rooms, etc. Thus, God has given us the ministry of helps, the Deacons, to do the everyday work of running the church, freeing the Elders to do what they are called to do.

The Widows

And in those days, when the number of the disciples was multiplied, there arose a murmuring of the Grecians against the Hebrews, because their widows were neglected in the daily ministration. (Acts 6:1)

Honor widows that are widows indeed. But if any widow have children or nephews, let them learn first to shew piety at home, and to requite their parents: for that is good and acceptable before God. Now she that is a widow indeed, and desolate, trusteth in God, and continueth in supplications and prayers night and day. But she that liveth in pleasure is dead while she liveth. And these things give in charge, that they may be blameless. But if any provide not for his own, and specially for those of his own house, he hath denied the faith, and is worse than an infidel. Let not a widow be taken into the number under threescore years old, having been the wife of one man. Well reported of for good works; if she have brought up children, if she have lodged strangers, if she have washed the saints' feet, if she have relieved the afflicted, if she have diligently followed every good work. But the younger widows refuse: for when they have begun to wax wanton against Christ, they will marry; Having damnation, because they have cast off their first faith. And withal they learn to be idle, wandering about from house to house; and not only idle, but tattlers also and busybodies, speaking things which they ought not. I will therefore that the younger women marry, bear children, guide the house, give none occasion to the adversary to speak reproachfully. For some are already turned aside after Satan. If any man or woman that believeth have widows, let them relieve them, and let not the church be charged; that it may relieve them that are widows indeed. (1 Timothy 5:3-16)

Anyone who has an elderly relative knows that, financially, things can be very difficult for older people. Even if they have pensions or receive Social Security benefits, etc., making ends meet is often impossible. We all remember being horrified at reports of senior citizens eating dog food because they couldn't afford to buy food meant for human consumption. Unfortunately, such things are all too common in the United States, as well as in other countries.

The early church believed it was their responsibility to provide for the elderly Saints who could no longer provide for themselves. So it should be today: No elderly member of an Apostolic church should ever have to eat dog food or live in a cardboard box under a bridge!

The scriptures at the beginning of this chapter refer only to widows, with no mention of widowers. It should not be assumed that the church has no obligation toward elderly men. The scriptures refer only to widows because of the lifestyle prevalent in those days: A woman generally married before she turned seventeen. Brides as young as twelve years of age were not uncommon. A man, on the other hand, was usually over thirty before he married. This age difference of fifteen to twenty years meant that a woman almost always outlived her husband by many years. Therefore, elderly women with no means of support were quite common. Men usually worked their entire lives. Elderly men who could not work might turn to begging, but were far outnumbered by widows.

Today, people of both sexes generally retire when they reach a certain age. Sometimes they are forced to retire. Pensions and Social Security benefits are rarely enough to provide a proper living. Should they become too frail to live on their own, nursing homes are available, but are usually very expensive, and may demand every penny the elderly person receives.

Since both men and women may find themselves unable to support themselves when they get older, the church's obligation extends from widows to include widowers, and in fact, all elderly (and even disabled) Saints. If they meet the proper requirements (more on that in a moment), the church should supplement their pension, Social Security, etc., so that they are able to meet their expenses (food, rent, utilities, etc.). the church is unable to do this, another option is for the elderly Saint to become part of another Saint's household. Whatever method is used, no elderly Saint should ever be homeless, or without proper food, or without heat, electricity, etc.

Read the words of Jesus in Matthew 25:31-46!

1 Timothy 5:9 tells us that no widow under threescore (sixty) years of age should be "taken into the number." What Paul is saying here is that no widow under the age of sixty was to be supported financially by the church. Obviously, if a Saint under that age is disabled and unable to work, the church should not be negligent in offering support.

 n order to be accepted for church support, the

following conditions apply:

1.   At least 60 years of age

2.   Must trust in God and be regular in prayer

3.   Known for good works

4.   Have faithfully raised their children (if any)

5.   Have been hospitable to strangers

6.   Have washed the Saints' feet

7.   Have given to the poor

Note that if someone meeting these qualifications has children, grand-children, nieces or nephews who are in the church, those relatives are obligated to provide support, rather than the church. If they refuse, they are, according to scripture, worse than unbelievers. (1 Tim. 5:4,8,16) In such a case, the church will have to provide the support.

If a Saint becomes too frail to live alone, and requires skilled nursing care, the church may arrange for such care. Placement in a nursing facility should be a last option. The church has an obligation to ensure that the facility takes proper care of the elderly Saint, and that all his/her needs are properly met. If a church has many elderly Saints, it may consider opening a private home for them. States generally regulate such facilities, so check with State and local governments before opening such a facility.

The Children

Train up a child in the way he should go: and when he is old, he will not depart from it. (Proverbs 22:6)

Teaching the children the ways of the Lord is not only the parents' responsibility; it is also the church's. Children and teenagers in the church need to be taught the Word of God and how to live as Christian people.

This brings us to the Sunday School department. (Although this is a modern title, the concept of teaching the children the ways of God is certainly biblical.) The most important responsibility of the Elders in regard to this is appointing a Sunday School Superintendent. This is an Elder, someone who is faithful, spiritually mature, full of the Holy Ghost, who loves and understands children, and is dedicated to teaching them the ways of God. Once such a person has been appointed, s/he should set up the Sunday School department, and the Bishop and other Elders should not need to do anything more.

How does the newly-appointed Sunday School Superintendent go about setting up a Sunday School department? The first thing to do is choose Teachers. How many Teachers depends upon the number of children to be taught. The Superintendent needs to seek out established Saints, well versed in scripture, full of the Holy Ghost, apt to teach, and good with children. Teachers are part of the five-fold ministry described in Eph. 4:11. Whether those instructed are a roomful of first-graders, or the entire congregation of Saints, Teachers are charged with instructing them in the ways of truth.

Sunday School classes are usually given names like Toddlers, Beginners, Juniors, etc. Each class represents a particular age group. For example, the Juniors are usually children ages 9-11. It is important for the Sunday School to have "children's church" in addition to the regular activities and lessons planned by the teachers. Children's church is a worship service specifically for children. Its goal is to teach children to be comfortable in a church service, how to behave, how to worship, how to minister to each other, etc. Every few weeks, instead of children's church, the Sunday School may attend the adult service, and the children should be encouraged to participate as much as they are able. If the Sunday School has a choir that usually sings in children's church, this choir might also sing in the adult service occasionally, and might even sing with the adult choir.

Children's church isn't a game, although the children should be helped to understand that worship is a joyful experience. Church should be fun and exciting for them, as it is for us, but serious nevertheless. Children can receive the Holy Ghost in children's church, with only other children, and maybe a teacher, praying with them. Children who receive the Holy Ghost are ready for their Pastor to baptize them in water. In most cases, parental consent should be obtained before water baptism. There are exceptions to this. In the case of teens whose parents may be hostile to the church and the salvation message, it may be advisable to baptize them without parental knowledge and consent. The Pastor and Bishop should seek the Lord for wisdom in such cases. We know that God's laws supersede man's, and in cases of conflict between the Bible and human governments, the Bible is to be obeyed rather than the government. This applies in principle to conflicts between the Bible and parents, as well. The Bible commands water baptism. If a young person has received the Holy Ghost, and is capable of giving consent, s/he should probably be baptized.

One final word in relation to the children: In the church today, there is often a tendency to overlook or dismiss the children because of their youth. This is a mistake. While they are young, and often immature, that has never stopped God from using children. In the early 20th century, it was not uncommon for God to call Apostolic people in their early teens, or even younger, and give them an anointing to preach. If a child in the church today shows an aptitude for preaching or teaching, or is used in a spiritual gift, it's not "cute" or amusing: It's a God-given talent and calling that should be nurtured, and that child must be guided and allowed to grow in that ministry. Too often, this does not happen, and the results are not good: Some 35 years ago, there was a boy of five who received the Holy Ghost in church service. He was born to dedicated Apostolic parents, and had attended church since birth. Five is a bit young to receive the Holy Ghost, for most. But there was no question in anyone's mind that this boy had received this precious Gift, and understood it. Thus, he became the youngest person that church ever baptized in Jesus' name. It was clear immediately that this child was special. He began to see visions of angels, and he would describe what he saw to his parents. It is likely that this child would have gone on to a powerful ministry, if the church had handled him properly. But too many in the church just thought he was "cute," a bit precocious, perhaps. They overlooked the significance of what had happened to him. As a result, he grew up without anyone encouraging him or nurturing him in his gifts. After a while, he was just another boy in the Sunday School, and to this day, has not entered any type of ministry. Each child is precious, and each child has a place and function in the body. It is the duty of the Sunday School department to help each child find that place and function, no matter what it might be.

Worship Services and the Music Ministry

And in that day there shall be a root of Jesse, which shall stand for an ensign of the people; to it shall the Gentiles seek: and his rest shall be glorious. (Isaiah 11:10)

For precept must be upon precept, precept upon precept; line upon line, line upon line; here a little, and there a little: For with stammering lips and another tongue will he speak to this people. To whom he said, This is the rest wherewith ye may cause the weary to rest; and this is the refreshing: yet they would not hear. But the word of the LORD was unto them precept upon precept, precept upon precept; line upon line, line upon line; here a little, and there a little; that they might go, and fall backward, and be broken, and snared, and taken. (Isaiah 28:10-13)

Him that is weak in the faith receive ye, but not to doubtful disputations. For one believeth that he may eat all things: another, who is weak, eateth herbs. Let not him that eateth despise him that eateth not; and let not him which eateth not judge him that eateth: for God hath received him. Who art thou that judgest another man's servant? to his own master he standeth or falleth. Yea, he shall be holden up: for God is able to make him stand. One man esteemeth one day above another: another esteemeth every day alike. Let every man be fully persuaded in his own mind. He that regardeth the day, regardeth it unto the Lord; and he that regardeth not the day, to the Lord he doth not regard it. He that eateth, eateth to the Lord, for he giveth God thanks; and he that eateth not, to the Lord he eateth not, and giveth God thanks. For none of us liveth to himself, and no man dieth to himself. For whether we live, we live unto the Lord; and whether we die, we die unto the Lord: whether we live therefore, or die, we are the Lord's. For to this end Christ both died, and rose, and revived, that he might be Lord both of the dead and living. (Romans 14:1-9)

I was in the Spirit on the Lord's day, and heard behind me a great voice, as of a trumpet. (Rev. 1:10)

See also Psalms 149 and 150.

In the first century, the church all met together on the Sabbath. There are a couple of things Apostolic believers need to know about the Sabbath. First of all, the Sabbath is Saturday, not Sunday. There are some churches that tell us that because Jesus rose from the dead on Sunday morning, the Sabbath changed to Sunday. There is no place in the scripture where we can find such a teaching. New Testament reference to the Lord's Day refers to Saturday, not Sunday.

Keeping the Sabbath was a commandment given to the Jewish people, *not* to the Gentiles. It was the day of "rest," and was a shadow of something to come. The scriptures above show that the prophet Isaiah associated the concept of "rest" with the coming of Messiah and with the baptism of the Holy Ghost. In fact, he specifically identified the baptism of the Holy Ghost (stammering lips and another tongue) as the "rest" in Isaiah 28:10-13. Many times, what was done physically in the Old Testament is done spiritually in the New. So it is with the "rest": In the Old Testament, the Jewish people kept the seventh day, Saturday, as a day of rest. In the New Testament, the church was given a new "rest," i.e., the baptism of the Holy Ghost. This "rest" replaces the day of rest of the Old Testament, just as the sacrifice of Jesus on the cross replaced the sacrifice of animals in the Temple. The church is not obligated to regard one day above the others. (Some in the first century church, particularly Jews who had grown up keeping the Sabbath, continued to do so, but were warned not to judge others who did not keep it. Romans 14:1-9)

The Gentile church, after falling into doctrinal error, "changed" the Sabbath to Sunday in an effort to distance themselves from Judaism. This hastened the development of Christianity as a religion separate from Judaism, rather than a fulfillment of Judaism. The scriptures teach us, however, that we are spiritual heirs to Abraham, and they never suggest that Christianity is separate from Judaism. The fact that a backslidden church declared Sunday to be the Sabbath did not actually make Sunday the Sabbath. The Sabbath remains Saturday. Nevertheless, Sunday has come to be regarded as a Christian day of worship, and since many places of business are closed on Sunday, it does make it a convenient day for the church to meet. Since the church is not bound by the Sabbath, it does not matter which day we choose to meet together. Since many are accustomed to using Sunday for this purpose, it makes sense to continue to do so.

Most Apostolic churches hold two worship services on Sunday. The number and times of services should be determined by the Elders, based upon the needs of the congregation. In some very small churches, two Sunday services, while spiritually desirable, may be impractical. If the Bishop or Elders have secular employment on Sundays, two services may be impossible. Again, the Elders should know what is best for the church and should decide the service schedule accordingly.

In new, very small churches, the Bishop might need to arrange every detail of the services, from what songs will be sung, who will sing solos, what announcements need to be made, to what will be preached. In larger churches, worship leaders can attend to many of these things. Larger churches should have at least three or four worship leaders. A worship leader should be full of the Holy Ghost, living a good Christian life, and should have some musical ability and the grace to lead the people in praise and worship.

This brings us to the music ministry. This ministry must be effective, and not just entertaining. An experienced minister can discern when the music ministry is effective by the response of the congregation to the word of God: An inspired and anointed message will be ineffective unless the hearers are prepared to receive it. The thanksgiving, praise and worship should prepare the congregation spiritually to hear, receive, understand, and respond to the word of God. All who minister in the worship service should have a clear vision of what they are to accomplish.

For example: A worship leader who focuses on the music, the beat, the hype and the response of the congregation, can never be effective. The song leader must learn how to lead the congregation into the presence of God, and to lead them to open their spirits to the word of God. The effective worship leader will bring all the attention upon the Lord and not upon the music or the musicians. If each musician is struggling for attention, the Lord is not worshiped and the people are not prepared to hear the word of God.

The deception is that if the people are jumping and shouting and clapping, that constitutes praise and worship. It may... or it may only indicate that the people are in the flesh. It is very important to understand *why* we worship the way we do!

Our direction in worship is to corporately praise and exalt the Lord in spirit and in truth. Our aim is to avoid the trap of secular professionalism and human arrogance based on talents and gifting. We embrace using all Biblical forms and expressions of praise. We believe that the worship experience is a way that we, as a body, can obey the greatest commandment: The greatest commandment is to love God with all our heart, soul, mind and strength (Mark 12:30). The bible clearly shows that God is on the lookout for true worshipers:

But the hour is coming, and now is, when the true worshipers will worship the Father in spirit and truth; for the Father is seeking such to worship Him. John 4:23 (NASB)

The Father is looking for true worshipers: Those who will worship Him in spirit and in truth! To worship in spirit is to worship sincerely and by the leading of Holy Ghost. To worship in truth is to worship according to the principles of the Word (John 17:17) and the person of Jesus Christ (John 14:6). The goal in all our meetings is for the Father to find *us* in His search for true worshipers.

Our focus in worship should be praising God the way He wants to be praised, rather than the way we want, or are comfortable praising Him. Our selection of songs and music should be based on their content and message, and not necessarily on the way they play on human emotions.

God's pattern for worship is the praise which took place in David's tabernacle (1 Chron. 15:1, 16, 28-29; 16:4-6). God said in Amos 9:11 that He would restore this type of worship. We see this begin to be fulfilled with the early church:

After this I will return, and will build again the tabernacle of David, which is fallen down; and I will build again the ruins thereof, and I will set it up: That the residue of men might seek after the Lord, and all the Gentiles, upon whom my name is called, saith the Lord, who doeth all these things. Acts 15:16-17 (KJV)

Biblical worship, which was the worship of the

Apostolic New Testament church, includes:

> Singing *(Ps. 33:3; 47:6; 95:1)*

> Lifting the voice *(Ps. 26:7; 66:8)*

> Shouting *(Ps. 47:1, 5; 5:11)*

> Clapping hands *(Ps. 47:1)*

> Lifting hands *(Ps. 63:4; 134:2; 141:2; 143:6)*

> Kneeling *(Ps. 95:6)*

> Standing *(Ps. 24:3, Ps. 135:2, Rev. 15:2)*

➤   Musical instruments *(Ps. 150:3-5)*

➤   Dancing *(Ps. 30:11; 149:3; 150:4; 2 Sam. 6:14)*

Our goal should be to follow the example of the early church and devote ourselves to praising God (Acts 2:42, 47).

There are seven Hebrew words which are translated "praise" in the Old Testament.

ידה **Yadah**[2] This word, used 114 times in various forms, means to worship God with raised hands. It is believed to derive from the word יד "yad," which means "hand." I will praise (odeh) You, O LORD, with my whole heart; I will tell of all Your marvelous works. (Psalm 9:1) Let the peoples praise (yoducha)You, O God; Let all the peoples praise (yoducha) You. (Psalm 67:3)

תודה **Todah** This word, used 32 times in various forms, means to corporately worship God with raised hands. It is formed from the same root as yadah, but emphasizes the corporate aspect of worshiping God with extended hands. Some scholars believe this word describes the palms being face up in a position of expectancy to receive from God. Whoever offers praise (todah) glorifies Me; And to him who orders his conduct aright I will show the salvation of God. (Psalms 50:23) This word further takes in the concept of thanksgiving in worship, and in modern Hebrew, the word todah means "Thank you."

ברך **Barach** - This word, forms of which are used 325 times, means to worship God by kneeling in adoration. It is often translated "bless" and "kneel." ...And daily He shall be praised (y'varacheinhu) (Psalm 72:15). Bless (barachi) the LORD, O my soul; And all that is within me, bless His holy name! (Psalms 103:1) Oh come, let us worship and bow down; Let us kneel (nivr'chah) before the LORD our Maker (Psalms 95:6).

זמר **Zamar** This word, used 42 times in various forms, means to celebrate with musical instruments, accompanied by the voice (singing). To the end that my glory may sing praise (y'zamercha) to You and not be silent. O LORD my God, I will give thanks to You forever (Psalms 30:12).

---

2   Hebrew words in the heading are the root forms. Those in parentheses are the specific forms used in each verse. Often these forms have pronominal endings attached, such as "hu," "cha," etc. These correspond to objective or possessive pronouns which, in English, exist as separate words.

Therefore I will give thanks to You, O LORD, among the Gentiles, And sing praises (azamer) to Your name (2 Sam. 22:50).

שבח **Shibach** This word, forms of which are used 11 times, means to praise the Lord with a loud voice. Because Your lovingkindness is better than life, My lips shall praise (y'shabchuncha) You (Psalms 63:3).

הלל **Hilel** This word, used 166 times in various forms, means to boast, and thus be (clamorously - a noisy shouting, a loud continuous noise) foolish; to celebrate; to cause to appear foolish or stupid; praise; rave; rage; to act madly or act like a madman. It's plural imperative form, halelu, is the source of "Hallelujah" a Hebrew expression which means, "Praise the Lord" (or Praise Yah). I will praise (ahalelah) the name of God with a song, And will magnify Him with thanksgiving (Psalms 69:30). Let them praise (y'halelu) His name with the dance; Let them sing praises to Him with the timbrel and harp (Psalms 149:3). Praise (haleluhu) Him with the timbrel and dance; Praise (haleluhu) Him with stringed instruments and flutes (Psalms 150:4)!

תהילה **Tehilah** This word, forms of which are used 57 times, means to praise with singing. It is also the Hebrew word for *psalm*. Praise the LORD! Sing to the LORD a new song, And His praise (tehilato) in the assembly of saints (Psalms 149:1). We will not hide them from their children, Telling to the generation to come the praises (tehilot) of the LORD, And His strength and His wonderful works that He has done (Psalms 78:4).

When all the ministries are focused upon exalting and magnifying the Lord, praise and worship will be the result. In a nightclub, it is normal for all the attention to be upon the musicians, the music and the beat, but that is not effective in a worship service. Worship is not a "performance" or a "show" or a "concert." When the music ministry "performs," focus, and ultimately worship, is taken away from the Lord and directed toward them. Such "worship" may be fun, but is spiritually meaningless. In addition, competition between those who minister in music always points to self-centered, self-exalting carnal natures, and will be an ineffective ministry. When the focus is on self, rather than on the Lord, failure is always the result, no matter how much the people run and shout. (Of course, this holds true for all ministers. No minister who seeks to be exalted will be effective for the Kingdom, no matter how many people flock to hear him/her.)

To see how a worship leader performs his/her duty, let us return to our hypothetical church in Poli. The Bishop, Brother Stephanos, approached one of the seven worship leaders on the Sabbath morning, and asked him to take the service next Saturday morning. (The Poli church, being Gentile, did not have any history of Sabbath-keeping, but chooses to meet on the Sabbath because their Jewish Christian neighbors in the nearby city of "Ir" [Hebrew for *city*] meet on the Sabbath. They are simply following an example, rather than actually considering one day above another.) Brother Stephanos then approached another worship leader, and asked her to take the service next Saturday evening.

During the week, both worship leaders spent much time in prayer, seeking God for His will for the services. In addition, both spent time with the musicians, practicing, praying and worshiping with them. Saturday morning, before service, the first worship leader, who we'll call Brother Timothy, and the rest of the music ministry, arrived at the meeting hall early to pray. With the guidance of the Spirit, they chose the songs the congregation would sing that morning. As the Saints began to arrive, Brother Timothy spoke briefly with the various Deacons, Pastors, and department heads (Sunday School, etc.), as well as with the Bishop, to determine what announcements needed to be made. He also asked one of the Saints if she would sing a solo, and spoke with the choir director to determine if the choir would be singing.

When the time for service came, the Saints gathered in the Sanctuary. Actually, many of them were already in there, praying. Others were in various other parts of the building, also praying. When the Saints had gathered, Brother Timothy stood in the pulpit and asked the Saints to stand and worship with him. After a few minutes of worship, he read a verse from the scripture, calling on the people to praise the Lord. More spontaneous worship followed. Then he made the announcements and began to lead the congregation in singing the songs that were chosen. After each song, the church erupted in praise and worship. During one of the songs, Brother Timothy placed a basket in front of the pulpit, and the Saints brought their tithes and offerings to the Lord, still singing.

After about forty minutes of song and praise, Sister Joanna was asked to sing her solo. She sang a song that told of the emptiness in her life before she came to know the Lord, and how He had filled that emptiness. When she finished, the congregation rose spontaneously and began to worship. Suddenly, the whole room became quiet, and from somewhere in the back of the room, a Sister began to speak in tongues. After her message, another Saint delivered the interpretation, in which the Lord exhorted His people to remember the places He had brought them from, and reminded them of the multitudes still lost in those places, and of their obligation to those multitudes. There was a brief period of prayer, as the Saints responded to the message, and then Brother Timothy led them in a prayer of re-dedication to the task of reaching the lost. After the prayer, he asked the choir and their leader to come and sing. When the choir had finished singing, the congregation sang another song, during which the worship leader sat down and a Preacher came to the Pulpit. The Preacher finished leading the song, and then began to preach the Word.

A certain amount of flexibility is essential in leading a service. While Brother Timothy had a rough outline of what scripture he would read, what songs they would sing, etc., none of it was carved in stone (or printed in a bulletin, for that matter). Room was left for the Holy Ghost to move. Certainly the message in tongues and the interpretation were not planned ahead of time. ut when God did move that way, the worship leader was able to take the cue and follow the Spirit's leading.

In some services, the Holy Ghost takes over from the beginning, and nothing that the worship leader has planned ahead of time takes place. In one such service, after the worship leader had led one or two songs, the Lord spoke in prophecy, and the message was so powerful and so convicting, that the song service could not continue. Within minutes, the entire congregation was on its face before the Lord, weeping. All over the Sanctuary, Saints lay on the floor, or knelt next to pews. The spirit of conviction remained, and the Saints wept and prayed for hours. There was no song service, no solo, no choir, no offering, not even a sermon. One message from the Lord had taken over the entire service, and a powerful change was made in the lives of the people. But what would have happened if there had been no flexibility in the service? Can you imagine what would have happened if the worship leader had tried to follow up the message from God with the next song on his list? Or with the offering? There would have been confusion. The Spirit of God was working in the hearts of the Saints, and anything that interfered with it would have caused palpable confusion.

The church needs musicians. Whether it's a tiny church with one person picking out a melody on an out-of-tune piano, or a large church with a fifty piece orchestra, the church needs people who can play instruments. Psalm 150 teaches us that a wide range of instruments can be used. So whether it's an accordion, an electric guitar, a saxophone, a synthesizer, or even bagpipes, any musically gifted Saint who is living for God should be permitted, and encouraged, to play during the worship services. But it shouldn't stop there! Percussion instruments like tambourines, maracas, bells, etc., can be scattered throughout the sanctuary, so that some of the Saints can play along while others clap their hands. Psalm 98:4 and Psalm 100:1 both tell us to "Make a joyful noise unto the LORD!"

Financial Matters

Will a man rob God? Yet ye have robbed me. But ye say, Wherein have we robbed thee? In tithes and offerings. Ye are cursed with a curse: for ye have robbed me, even this whole nation. Bring ye all the tithes into the storehouse, that there may be meat in mine house, and prove me now herewith, saith the LORD of hosts, if I will not open you the windows of heaven, and pour you out a blessing, that there shall not be room enough to receive it. And I will rebuke the devourer for your sakes, and he shall not destroy the fruits of your ground; neither shall your vine cast her fruit before the time in the field, saith the LORD of hosts. And all nations shall call you blessed: for ye shall be a delightsome land, saith the LORD of hosts. (Malachi 3:8-12)

Who goeth a warfare any time at his own charges? who planteth a vineyard, and eateth not of the fruit thereof? or who feedeth a flock, and eateth not of the milk of the flock? Say I these things as a man? or saith not the law the same also? For it is written in the law of Moses, Thou shalt not muzzle the mouth of the ox that treadeth out the corn. Doth God take care for oxen? Or saith he it altogether for our sakes? For our sakes, no doubt, this is written: that he that ploweth should plow in hope; and that he that thresheth in hope should be partaker of his hope. If we have sown unto you spiritual things, is it a great thing if we shall reap your carnal things? If others be partakers of this power over you, are not we rather? Nevertheless we have not used this power; but suffer all things, lest we should hinder the gospel of Christ. Do ye not know that they which minister about holy things live of the things of the temple? and they which wait at the altar are partakers with the altar? Even so hath the Lord ordained that they which preach the gospel should live of the gospel. (1 Cor. 9:7-14)

Let the elders that rule well be counted worthy of double honor, especially they who labor in the word and doctrine. For the scripture saith, Thou shalt not muzzle the ox that treadeth out the corn. And, The laborer is worthy of his reward. (1 Tim. 5:17-18)

(The following is adapted from the tract "HOW MUCH SHOULD I GIVE? A Guide to Tithes And Offerings," reprinted by permission of Lighthouse Ministries.)

46

There is much confusion in the church world today on the subject of giving to the church. In some churches, throwing a dollar or two into the plate on Sunday morning is considered sufficient, while in others, all members are asked to pledge a certain amount per year. Amid the various customs, isn't there a biblical standard of giving that we may go by? Doesn't the scripture tell us what God expects of His people in this area? Most assuredly it does.

In discussing the subject of tithes and offerings, it needs to be made clear that we are not speaking only of money. While determining how much God expects us to give, let us remember that the very same standard applies to all areas of our lives, including our time and our talents. With that thought in mind, let us turn to the scriptures. The reader is very strongly urged to take the time right now to look up the following scriptures and to read each one carefully:

Gen. 28:20-22; Lev. 27:30; Num. 18:21; II Chron. 31:5; Neh. 13:12; Prov. 3:9-10; Deut. 25:4; Mt. 23:23

Let's talk about tithing first. What is a tithe? The word tithe means "one tenth." We can see from the above scriptures that God instructed Israel that they were to give one tenth of all their increase. This meant that one tenth of their crops, one tenth of their livestock, one tenth of their monetary income, and yes, one tenth of their time and abilities, belonged to the Lord. What was this one tenth to be used for? It was given to the priests and the Levites for them to live on. You see, when the promised land was divided up for the tribes of Israel, the tribe of Levi was given no portion. God told the priests and Levites that *He* was their portion, their inheritance. However, having no land meant that the Levites could not plant crops or raise animals. They had no means of support. There sole duty was to be attending to the things of God. And in return for their ministering, the people of Israel would support them by giving one tenth of their substance.

In the above scriptures, you'll also find the word "firstfruits." What does that mean? It means "off the top." That is, their one tenth was to be given first, before any of the income was used. God told them that the first one tenth belonged to Him. It was holy.

In the book of Malachi, God accused the people of Israel of stealing from Him. When they tried to protest their innocence and asked how He thought they had stolen from Him, He answered that they had stolen from Him by not paying their tithes. Several times in the history of the Jewish people, we see that they stopped paying tithes. The result was that the priests and Levites were forced to abandon the work of God and to go out and find secular jobs. The Temple fell into disrepair, and the word of God was neglected and forgotten. At one point in Judah's history, it had been so long since the word of God had been read, that when it was found and read to the king, he was horrified, because they were not living according to its teachings. In his whole life, he had never heard the word, because the Levites and priests were out trying to earn a living.

The scriptures of the Old Testament make certain points very clear: First, tithing was God's plan for the support of the ministry. Second, tithing was not optional; it was mandatory. The first one tenth, according to God belonged to Him, and to hold it back was stealing from God. (Malachi 3:8-12) A tithe is not an offering. An offering is a free-will gift. Anything given after tithes are paid is an offering. While God promises innumerable blessings to tithers, even greater blessings are given to those who give more of their own free will. (2 Cor. 9:7)

But what about the New Testament? It is clear that tithing was the correct system in the Old Testament, but is it still in effect? When searching the New Testament for an answer to this question, one thing we cannot fail to notice is that, while tithing isn't taught directly, no other system was ever instituted. The Apostles, who were all raised in the Jewish faith, had always tithed as a matter of course. There is no indication that they ever abandoned this habit. When the Gentiles entered the church, they modeled their churches after the Jewish Christian churches. Undoubtedly, they began to tithe as well.

We read in the above scriptures that Jesus berated the Pharisees for paying tithes but neglecting the more important aspects of the Law. In other words, they had the letter of the law (such as tithing), but lacked the spirit of the law, things like mercy and justice. But notice that Jesus didn't tell them they shouldn't have paid their tithes. He told them that they should indeed have done what they did, that is, tithed, but they should not have neglected the other things. In other words, He expected them both to tithe *and* be merciful.

We have also included above three verses of scripture that talk about not muzzling an ox who is treading the corn. What is that all about? This is an indication of how God expects the ministry to be supported. Under the Law of Moses, an ox who turned a mill to grind corn was not to be muzzled. This meant that the ox was free to eat any of the corn that spilled out in front of him. This was his pay, since he was the one who turned the mill. This was used in the New Testament to show how God planned for the ministers of the Gospel to be supported. In 1 Cor. 9:13-

14, we see that God expects those who labor in the Gospel to derive their support from it. Any church, once it has grown to a certain size, should be able to pay their Bishop a salary so that s/he may have the ability to minister fully to them, rather than having to devote the time to secular employment. And let's face it, a dollar or two a week in the collection plate is not going to pay the rent or mortgage, keep the lights, heat, air conditioning and water turned on, nor will it pay for printing tracts, buying Bibles and songbooks, put food on the Bishop's table, pay his or her rent and utilities, or put gas in his or her car. And two hours of your time to sit in service won't mow the church lawn or paint the Sunday School rooms. Who will do those things? Why the Bishop, right after s/he gets out of work!

"Oh, but you just don't understand my financial situation! I can't afford to pay tithes!" Neither can I. But on the other hand, I can't afford not to! That ten percent belongs to God already, and if I choose to keep it, then I am a thief. And if I am honest. I will acknowledge that if it weren't for the grace of God, I would have no income at all. How, then, can I keep it back from Him? If He asked for the full 100%, I would still have no choice but to give it to Him. It would still be little enough to ask from me, when I consider what He gave for me. And I'll tell you a little secret: If you make the sacrifice and pay your ten percent off the top, before paying anything else, the 90% that remains will stretch further than the 100% ever would have! How? I guess the best answer is found in Malachi 3:10.

Don't forget your time and talents! Ten percent are God's. Can't you give a few hours a week to help clean the church? Or a few hours to go out witnessing to others about Jesus? Or how about asking the Pastor or Bishop if there are some errands you can run so that the man or woman of God is free to spend some time in prayer or in the word? Do you have musical talent? If so, why not use it for the Kingdom? Do you have writing ability? Why not write a short article on events in your local church for a church newsletter? Everyone has abilities that can be used for the glory of God, if they're willing to use them.

"Give and it shall be given unto you; good measure, pressed down, and shaken together, and running over, shall men give into your bosom. For with the same measure that ye mete withal it shall be measured to you again." Lk. 6:38

After reading the above, you should have an idea of how tithes and offerings work, and what God expects of His people in this area. Running a church can be very expensive, and if the Saints don't tithe, it will be impossible for the church to operate properly.

What are some of the expenses involved in church administration? This depends on the size of the church. The larger the church, the more expenses it will have. Here are some expenses a church might have: Rent or mortgage payment for the church building, utilities (heat, air conditioning, electricity, telephone, water, sewer, etc.), office supplies, computer equipment, furniture (pews are very expensive), building maintenance, janitorial supplies, postage, advertising costs, and salaries. These are just a few possible expenses. There may be many more. (For example, if the Sunday School uses buses to transport children to and from church, there will be gasoline, maintenance, insurance, etc., to consider.)

On the subject of salaries, two things need to be discussed: First, who is entitled to a salary, and second, how much should they be paid? It has already been mentioned that the Bishop should be paid a salary. The scriptures at the beginning of this chapter indicate that God expects those who labor in the Gospel to derive their living from it. This means other ministers in the church should also receive some type of salary. (More on that in a moment.) What about Deacons? It depends on what they're doing and for how many hours. Any Deacon working full time, for example, the Secretary, should receive a salary. Deacons who only work a few hours a week, such as ushers, probably have other employment, and shouldn't need any pay. Treasurers, Sunday School Superintendents, etc., might warrant a salary if they are actually working a significant number of hours. In such cases, rather than a specific salary, they might be paid for the hours they actually work.

What about the ministers? Of course the Bishop gets a salary. What about a Teacher? If there is a licensed or ordained minister whose call is Teacher, s/he should be paid. If the teaching is done in a Bible school, the school should pay a salary. If the teaching is done in a church, the church should pay something. Unless the Teacher is actually teaching full time, a full time salary is not warranted.

Prophets don't generally minister full time in that calling, and, unless the Holy Ghost instructs otherwise, probably should not receive a salary. If a Prophet does minister full time, or has another call in addition to Prophet, a salary may be warranted.

An Evangelist should receive some type of salary from his/her home church. In addition, an Evangelist should receive some type of love offering from any church s/he preaches in, commensurate with the size of the church and what they are able to afford. (A very small church may only be able to afford a very few dollars, while a large church could afford much more. The Evangelist should not be concerned with the size of the offering, but should minister equally to churches of all sizes and financial means.)

What about the Apostles? Since the Apostle doesn't actually have a home church, his/her support comes in a different way. Every church of any size should "adopt" an Apostle, and pledge to send him/her an offering each month. A minimum offering should be specified, even if it's just ten dollars a month. (They can always send more if they wish.) Larger churches should adopt as many Apostles as they can reasonably afford, and pledge a monthly offering to each. Also, it wouldn't hurt for the Apostles to have some kind of vocational training to provide a supplementary income. (Paul made tents when he wasn't preaching.)

A church that adopts an Apostle should display a picture of the Apostle (and his/her spouse, if any) in the church building, along with some information about the area where the Apostle is currently working. It is important for the Saints to feel some connection to the Apostles they're helping to support. Whenever the Lord permits, an Apostle should visit the churches that have adopted him/her.

How much should the Bishop be paid? There is more than one way to determine this. Some churches set a specific yearly salary, while others give the Bishop ten percent of whatever the church takes in. Either system is acceptable, provided that the Bishop is paid a sufficient amount to live on. If the church does not have a parsonage, the Bishop will likely need to rent a place to live, and that needs to be taken into account when determining salary. Who makes the decision? Actually, the Bishop does. We disapprove of "Church Boards" that make such decisions in some churches. The church is not a dictatorship under the control of a Board, nor a democracy where the congregation should vote.

Rather, the church is a theocracy, where God rules, and has placed the Bishop over the church. A man or woman called to be a Bishop may be trusted not to steal from the church or to take more than s/he is entitled to. Any Bishop who would mishandle the church's money in any way may be assured that God will intervene on the church's behalf. (See Jer. 12:10-11; 23:1-3)

An example for all Bishops is Brother S. R. Hanby, who was an Apostle. In the many churches he opened, he always used the same standard for determining how much he would be paid while he was Bishop of the new work. In each church, he was entitled to ten percent of what the church took in. (In a very small, new church, that might be only a dollar or two a week!) BUT, Brother Hanby never took that ten percent: He took only a fraction of it, just enough to live on. He worked sixty to eighty hours a week for the church, but always looked for ways to decrease the amount of money he would need to live on. For example, he planted a garden and grew most of his food. But there's more: Of the small fraction of his salary that he actually did take, Brother Hanby gave ten percent of it back to the church: He tithed.

We've all seen millionaire preachers on TV telling us they need another million dollars to stay on the air. They drive big cars, wear expensive suits, live in mansions and wear flashy jewelry. Then there are preachers like Brother Hanby, who wore modestly priced clothes, grew his own food, drove an old car until it fell apart, and gave every spare dime to the work of God. Some preachers choose to live in mansions here on earth. Others prefer to store their treasure in heaven instead. Someday, Brother Hanby will have a mansion all the money on earth couldn't buy, built alongside a street paved with purest gold!

Trouble in the Church

Moreover if thy brother shall trespass against thee, go and tell him his fault between thee and him alone: if he shall hear thee, thou hast gained thy brother. But if he will not hear thee, then take with thee one or two more, that in the mouth of two or three witnesses every word may be established. And if he shall neglect to hear them, tell it unto the church: but if he neglect to hear the church, let him be unto thee as an heathen man and a publican. (Matthew 18:15-17)

And early in the morning he came again into the temple, and all the people came unto him; and he sat down, and taught them. And the scribes and Pharisees brought unto him a woman taken in adultery; and when they had set her in the midst, They say unto him, Master, this woman was taken in adultery, in the very act. Now Moses in the law commanded us, that such should be stoned: but what sayest thou? This they said, tempting him , that they might have to accuse him. But Jesus stooped down, and with his finger wrote on the ground, as though he heard them not. So when they continued asking him, he lifted up himself, and said unto them, He that is without sin among you, let him first cast a stone at her. And again he stooped down, and wrote on the ground. And they which heard it, being convicted by their own conscience, went out one by one, beginning at the eldest, even unto the last: and Jesus was left alone, and the woman standing in the midst. When Jesus had lifted up himself, and saw none but the woman, he said unto her, Woman, where are those thine accusers? hath no man condemned thee? She said, No man, Lord. And Jesus said unto her, Neither do I condemn thee: go, and sin no more. (John 8:2-11)

Brethren, if a man be overtaken in a fault, ye which are spiritual, restore such an one in the spirit of meekness; considering thyself, lest thou also be tempted. (Gal. 6:1)

Rebuke not an elder, but entreat him as a father; and the younger men as brethren; The elder women as mothers; the younger as sisters, with all purity... Against an elder receive not an accusation, but before two or three witnesses. Them that sin rebuke before all, that others also may fear. (1 Tim. 5:1-2,19-20)

A man that is a heretic after the first and second admonition reject; Knowing that he that is such is subverted, and sinneth, being condemned of himself. (Titus 3:10-11)

One of the most uncomfortable topics for most ministers is the matter of church discipline, when someone in the church has done something wrong, and corrective action must be taken. There are three areas of church discipline we need to look at: First, interpersonal disputes and offenses, in which one Saint has deliberately done something to hurt another. Second is the matter of the Saint who has fallen into sin. Finally, we need to look at the matter of heretics, that is, church members who preach false doctrine.

Perhaps the best way to examine the subject of interpersonal disputes and offenses is to look at an actual example. The following is a condensed version of a true story. The names of all involved have been changed.

Sister Betty was the leader of a church youth group. Brother Smith and Brother Black were "co-Pastors" of the church. In private conference, Brother Smith gave Sister Betty permission for the youth group to meet Sunday afternoons in one of the Sunday School rooms for prayer. However, on the second Sunday that the youth group did so, Brother Smith interrupted the prayer meeting, and took Sister Betty out into the hall. He told her that he had never given permission for the meetings. Sister Betty was confused, but said nothing. She asked the youth group to remember to pray for both Pastors, and dismissed the meeting.

Brother Smith began to contact the parents of some of the youth group members, and told them that Sister Betty was speaking against him at the youth group's regular Friday night meetings. The accusation was untrue, but several parents pulled their children out of the group, and began to shun Sister Betty at church. Had not some of the youth group members told Sister Betty what Brother Smith had said, she might never have known why people were treating her differently.

Sister Betty had heard the same report from several of the teens, and even a few of the parents. She asked Brother Smith about it privately, as the scripture instructs, but he denied everything.

On a Sunday morning shortly afterward, Brother Smith arrived at church obviously upset about something. (Brother Black was out of town at a ministers' conference.) Twice during service, Brother Smith stopped the singing, saying that people weren't keeping up with him. The second time, he also snapped at the organist, accusing her of playing too slowly.

Following this, he openly accused a Brother in the congregation of having an ugly spirit. He then turned to Sister Betty and verbally attacked her in front of her children and the church. He accused her of speaking against him and of hindering revival in the church. She quietly replied only that God was just and merciful, and the He would show who was telling the truth and who was not. Brother Smith shouted back that she was in trouble with God.

When Brother Black returned from the ministers' conference, Sister Betty went to see him with two other Saints. She told Brother Black what had been happening, and the other Saints confirmed her words. As scripture instructs, she brought two witnesses with her because her accusation was against an Elder. She asked Brother Black to arrange a meeting for her with both himself and Brother Smith, where the three of them might discuss the situation. This meeting would have been the next scriptural step in dealing with such a situation. Brother Smith, however, repeatedly refused Brother Black's requests for such a meeting. He would meet with Brother Black, he said, but not with Sister Betty. This left Brother Black with no choice but to take the matter to the church.

A special meeting of the congregation was called. Brother Black outlined the accusations Sister Betty had made, reminded the congregation of Brother Smith's verbal attack on her before the church, and told the church that he had repeatedly asked Brother Smith to meet with Sister Betty and himself to clear the matter up. He told the congregation that Brother Smith had refused every invitation.

At that point, Brother Smith was asked if he wished to say anything. He responded by repeating his earlier accusations against Sister Betty. He went on to say that Brother Black had never tried to arrange any meeting, but that he, himself, had tried to arrange such a meeting, but Sister Betty had refused to meet with him. He strongly implied that Brother Black was lying.

Now, Brother Black was a very old and respected minister, having been a preacher of the Gospel more than fifty years. At Brother Smith's insinuation that Brother Black was lying, the congregation was deeply shocked, and knew that something was wrong with Brother Smith's story. Brother Smith was removed from his position. He would have been welcome to stay in the church, but chose to leave and start another church.

It is, of course, a disgraceful thing that something like this should ever happen in the church. Nevertheless, Sister Betty handled the situation in the correct manner, according to scripture, and never, never said or did anything to or about Brother Smith that was less than Christian.

What should be done when a Brother or Sister falls into sin? Now, let's understand what we're talking about here: All of us sin occasionally. Any Saint who says s/he no longer sins at all is probably guilty of the sin of pride! We're still human and we make mistakes. But when we repent, the Lord is merciful and forgives us. We need also to understand that sin is sin. As far as God is concerned, there are not "big" sins and "little" sins. (Or as some categorize them, venial and mortal sins.) Lying, stealing, murder, fornication, gossip, slander, etc., all have equal ability to keep people out of the Kingdom of Heaven. And any one of those, if repented of, will be forgiven. When we're talking about Saints falling into sin, we're not talking about an occasional mistake followed by repentance. Rather, we're talking about sin that is not repented of, sin that is continually repeated, or sin that is publicly known and may bring shame to the work of God.

In many churches, if anyone is found guilty of sin, he or she is forced to leave the church. Churches like that generally categorize sin. Things like fornication and divorce are considered "serious" sins, and a minister found guilty of one of those may never be allowed to preach again! (Divorce is not always a sin, and under certain circumstances is permitted. Some churches treat it as sin nevertheless.) But as was mentioned above, God does not categorize sin. God forgives fornication as easily as lying. It's only people who have trouble forgiving!

Again, an actual example of a Brother who had fallen into sin will help us understand the proper response of the church. As in the previous story, all names have been changed.

Brother Bob was arrested in a department store. According to police, he had exposed himself to a woman in the store. He pleaded guilty, was ordered to get professional help, and was released into the custody of his wife and Pastor. The story was printed in the paper, and it became known that Brother Bob had been doing this kind of thing for quite a while. He was, however, repentant, and sought not only professional help, but help from his Pastor.

Brother Bob and his wife were, of course, very embarrassed and ashamed by what had happened, and were fearful of what type of reaction the church would have. They knew very well that many churches would throw them both out, or would treat them as "second class citizens." But what would *their* church do?

The next Sunday morning, Brother Bob and his wife walked through the front door of the church with their infant daughter. The first Saint who spotted them rushed over and hugged Brother Bob tightly. Others also came over, hugging Brother Bob and his wife. There were tears and words of love, but no mention of the sin and no words of judgment or condemnation. Brother Bob's wife later told one of the Saints how much it meant to Bob that the church responded as it did. Their unconditional love made it that much easier for him to overcome his problem. Had they responded differently to Brother Bob, both he and his wife might have been driven from the church by their attitudes, and might have given up on God.

This story had a happy ending. But suppose that Brother Bob had been unrepentant, and had tried to justify his sin. If the church did not deal with it, Brother Bob's sinning would no doubt continue, and he would no doubt be arrested again, and his rebuke would also fall on the church that knew of his actions but did nothing.

What should the church do with an unrepentant sinner? First, privately, the Pastor or Bishop should use scripture to show that the action in question is indeed sin. The Pastor or Bishop should then ask the person to stop the sinful activity. This needs to be done in love, not judgment, firmly, but not in an attitude of condemnation. (If the sin involves a problem such as the one Brother Bob had, just saying "stop sinning" will not be enough. Pastoral counseling, and perhaps professional help, will be needed. If this is the case, the Pastor or Bishop needs to indicate that during this meeting.) If the person agrees, and repents, then the matter is closed. If s/he agrees, but the activity continues, another meeting with the Bishop and two or three witnesses (established Saints, perhaps Pastors or Deacons, but not busybodies!) needs to be held. Once again, the scripture should be used to show that the action in question is sin, and the person should again be asked to repent and desist from the activity. (A Saint who is weak and is prone to sinning repeatedly may need extra help. Although the church can't reasonably be expected to provide "babysitting" service for an adult, it may be helpful to ask a more established Saint to take the weak one under his/her wing, and more or less "keep an eye on him/her.") If the sinner agrees to repent and desist from the sinful activity, then the matter is closed and shouldn't be mentioned again.

If the person continues in the action after the second meeting, and every reasonable effort has been made to help, the church needs to be told the whole matter. Now, what happens next is very important, and it's where many churches err. The scripture says that the offending person is to be treated as a heathen or a publican. Some churches interpret this to mean they should ostracize the person. He or she is thrown out of the church and is not spoken to again. But is that how Jesus treated heathens and publicans? Is that how the church is supposed to treat the lost? No!

Jesus spent much of His time with sinners, including unrepentant ones. He treated them with love, compassion, tolerance, understanding and respect. So it should be with the unrepentant sinner in the church. S/he should not be thrown out or ostracized. Unrepentant sinners are no longer addressed as Brother or Sister, since they're to be treated as though they were not yet part of the church. But just as any visitor to the church is warmly welcomed and given extra attention and love, so as to encourage them to repent, etc., so too, should the unrepentant sinner be treated in this manner. One of two things will happen: Either he or she will repent and will again be a part of the Family, or the unconditional love of the church will produce so much conviction that he or she will leave. But as long as there is any hope of repentance, the church must continue to love unconditionally.

Finally we come to the subject of heretics. A heretic is one who believes false doctrine. If the doctrine is something minor, unrelated to biblical truths, and is not preached to others, it possibly can be ignored. Even if the doctrine is something major, for example, belief in the doctrine of the Trinity, as long as the person keeps it to him/herself, it *may* cause no harm.

On the other hand, if anyone in the church begins to preach, teach, or otherwise pass on any false doctrine, action must be taken. Just as a little bit of yeast will leaven a whole loaf, a little bit of false doctrine can poison the whole church (See Gal. 5:7-9; Jude 1-25). The Pastor or Bishop should privately explain to the person why the doctrine is false, using scripture, and should warn him/her not to speak further of it to Saints or visitors. If the warning is heeded, the matter should be dropped.

If the situation continues, the Bishop, with two or three witnesses, should again explain why the doctrine is false, using scripture, and should repeat the warning. Again, if the warning is heeded, the matter should be dropped.

If the situation still continues, the scripture instructs us to "reject" the heretic. Reject means to throw away or discard. This is one of the few cases when it may be necessary to put someone out of the church. It is a sad thing, but necessary, because the teaching of false doctrine can destroy the unity of the Body, cause doctrinal dissension, and can seriously harm the work of God. Just as a cancerous body part must be removed if the cancer does not respond to treatment, so too must a heretic who will not heed the Bishop's warnings be removed from the church. In both cases, the survival of the Body depends on it.

Starting New Churches

Starting a new church is the work of the Apostle. As mentioned in an earlier chapter, an Apostle is equivalent to what we today call a missionary: Someone who goes to an area where the Gospel has not been preached, or where it has been preached in an incorrect form, and begins a new work there.

It needs to be emphasized that the work of an Apostle is STARTING a new church. If a man or woman who is called as an Apostle decides to stay with the new church and become the Bishop or a Pastor, then something may well be wrong. This is not the example set for us by the first century Apostles. Yes, some of the Apostles stayed with the Jerusalem church. Founding that church was their mission. But today, our better examples are Paul and Barnabas and people like them. They did what Apostles today need to do: Establish a new church, ordain Elders in the new church, and then move on to whatever place the Holy Ghost leads them to start over again.

This pattern hasn't often been followed by the modern church. One Apostle, who began opening new church works early in the 20th century, found it difficult to continue in that pattern once the Apostolic churches formed large denominations. For some reason, they didn't like to see a minister start a church, turn it over to someone else, and then move elsewhere to start a new one. Perhaps they thought it looked like instability. So this particular Apostle, now elderly, found a way around their objections: He retired as pastor of the church he had founded. He then moved to another state, reprinted all the tracts and opened a new church. Apparently, he "retired" in this fashion a few times!

If the Apostolic church were functioning properly, however, an Apostle wouldn't have to resort to such creative thinking to be able to move on. The church would *expect* the Apostle to move on.

Those who have started a new church, and then left to open another, will understand: The very real challenge is how to leave a church for which we have poured out our life in the hands of others, especially when the "others" are men and women who, like most or all of the saints in this new church, have only recently come to a knowledge of truth. This becomes a bit easier when we remember that the church does not belong to us: It belongs to Jesus. He said **He** would build **His** church, and the gates of Hell would not be able to prevail against it.

Once we understand that His pattern is to have the church led by a group of Elders, it releases us from the care and responsibility. That, in our view, some elders may seem inadequate in many areas is no longer relevant. We commend them into the grace of God, and give Him the control of His church. This brings us to the task of finding quality leaders.

We may have a relatively mature person whom we feel is gifted in several areas, and has great ability to preach and teach, but has no burden for the people. Others whom we would like to see raised up into leadership are not very faithful, or they are easily offended, or are inconsistent in other areas in their lives.

Some, who have some ability to speak, only speak on an elementary level, far below the comprehension or the experience of the assembly. Even in all this, we need to trust the leadership of the Holy Ghost or we will soon find that no one comes up to our standards of excellence!

We must believe that God will raise up the perfect replacement ministries so we can leave and pursue our calling. Everyone who has been called to start and extend the church is well aware of these problems, plus a hundred more. The problems are much too complex to solve now in a single move or by simply making a new policy or teaching a new doctrine. We could say, "the die is cast and we are stuck with it". However, we must ask the question: Does every new assembly that is raised up have to be cast with the same die? If we continue to do it our way, instead of God's, we will continue to see the same limited results. So the answer to the question depends on what we want to see. If we are content with what we have, we don't need to change. On the other hand, if we truly long to see the original Apostolic church, in all its power and effectiveness, restored in our midst, then change is essential.

An immature church can easily grow in maturity right along with an immature leadership. In this case being Elders is relative to the maturity of the assembly. Our problem is trying to find mature Elders to lead an assembly once the assembly has come to a certain measure of maturity. "Elders" presupposes that those ordained as such are more mature than the rest of the assembly.

61

How can we select Elders from a group of people who are all at the same level of maturity? Even though the assembly might accept these Elders, there is likely to be constant criticism. Everybody knows as much as everybody else, and some will think they know more that the "Elders".

In the early churches founded after the Jerusalem church, everybody started out equal. There were no transfers of "mature" believers from other churches like we have today. No one really had a clue about how things were to be established.

Paul and Timothy preached to some people, and some believed. After they had a few souls, they continued on with their ministry in other places. After some time had passed, they went back to see what God had done, and whom He had raised up.

When they found people whom the believers recognized as "elders," they laid hands on them and acknowledged what God had done. The church was then left in the hands of "Elders" who only a few months ago were worshiping heathen idols. Remember, they had no New Testaments to leave with the "Elders". In the new churches, everybody grew together.

We might well face these same problems in starting new works today. One consistent error is that we have may have raised up "a new church," but we have neglected to raise up elders of that church. Sometimes we may have to appoint elders by default. We may be required to appoint elders before we can incorporate, so we pick some who are more agreeable with us and our position. Some ministries even deliberately pick weak leaders, because they don't want anyone to confront them about things they are doing. If Elders are chosen for carnal reasons, such as popularity, good looks, charisma, etc., rather than for their gifts and calling and abilities, there will be serious, perhaps insurmountable, problems.

We see in 3 John that such an Elder, Diotrephes, was a detriment to the work there. He had an ego problem, liked to be in the limelight, and as a result, wouldn't allow any ministers around who might upstage him. Even John was not welcome to visit, and if any saint tried to welcome John or other visiting ministers, Diotrephes put them out of the church!

We like to think such things couldn't happen in our Apostolic churches today, but they do happen. And since Diotrephes was the Bishop there, John couldn't just go in and throw him out. They were stuck with him. So John realized that the only hope for the saints there was for a new work to start. His message is written between the lines of his epistle, so to speak. Just as he couldn't oust Diotrephes, he couldn't just say, "everybody stop going to church there, and we'll start a new one." Instead, he told them not to follow what was evil, but to follow what was good. Then, in a seeming change of subject, he brought up Demetrius, whom he said had a good report of all, and he himself bore witness to that. The message, although unstated, was clear: The saints should not follow Diotrephes, but rather Demetrius. This may well have led to a split in the church. But when there is an Elder who has control and is carnal, and some choose to follow that Elder, a split may be desirable. We certainly wouldn't want good, honest saints to continue to follow a corrupt leader.

It would be difficult and chaotic to suddenly change the whole structure of an established church that has been founded in the traditional form, having one (super)Pastor, and maybe an assistant Pastor. While we acknowledge that it is not God's original plan, the changes required to bring it into alignment with the original Apostolic church will need to be instituted carefully.

We may already have board members in order comply with State regulations for a non-profit organization, and we may have recognized elders who work side by side with the board and vote equally in all matters of business for the church. We can start from where we are, with what we have, and slowly begin to change the traditional mindset regarding ministry and church government.

Once we have planted a new church, we must endeavor to help others come into their calling and grow into the leaders that God wants them to be.

It is important to recognize that the administration of a church functions on a different plane than the government of the church. The administration would have to answer to the government of Elders, but need not be daily controlled by them. In other words, the daily decisions concerning bills, charity, supplies, youth, camp expense, etc. could be determined by the administration and not have to wait for a meeting of the Elders. This will eliminate the many cumbersome problems that arise when the Bishop and Pastors have to make all the administration decisions. The administration must have the freedom to administrate. In a new church, we must seek God for ongoing growth and development of new leaders in both areas of church leadership.

Qualifications of Elders

We, as leaders, are always looking to find and recognize strengths in others in the assembly. However, if we don't recognize our own weakness, we won't be able to recognize that God has put someone in our midst that has that strength. If we claim to have all strengths and no weaknesses, we will attempt to do everything ourselves until we finally collapse. Then whom do we turn to for prayer?

1 Timothy 3:1-13 gives us good insight into the requirements of elders, deacons and those who oversee, but not much insight into job descriptions or the effectiveness of their function.

Paul says to test them by letting them function as deacons first. If they are ineffective as deacons, they will also be ineffective as elders. Since deacon simply means "servant," we watch for those who are quick to serve. If they are too busy to serve as deacons, undoubtedly they will be too busy, and ineffective, as elders.

Another thing to consider is how the role of Elders relates to overall ministry in the church. Remember that there are two practical aspects to government in the Church. There is the administrative side, and then there is the ministry, or spiritual side. Both are essential in the church, but they are separate functions.

We have heard that an Elder should be able and equipped to teach. But does an elder who functions only in the administrative side of church government also need to be qualified to teach in the spiritual function of ministry? In other words, we can divide the Elders into those two specific categories. There will be elders who function primarily in the spiritual areas of teaching and preaching; others will function in the areas of administration. An elder who is very effective in administration may not be able to teach.

And God has appointed in the church, first apostles, second prophets, third teachers, then miracles, then gifts of healings, helps, administrations, {vari-

ous} kinds of tongues. All are not apostles, are they? All are not prophets, are they? All are not teachers, are they? All are not {workers of} miracles, are they? All do not have gifts of healings, do they? All do not speak with tongues, do they? All do not interpret, do they? 1 Corinthians 12:28 (NASB)

This surely points to a diversity of ministries, each functioning in its own unique way.

Now there are varieties of gifts. but the same Spirit. And there are varieties of ministries, and the same Lord. And there are varieties of effects, but the same God who works all things in all persons. 1 Corinthians 12:4-6 (NASB)

It is clear from these scriptures that God has set gifts of administration in His church for the day-today issues that need handling, and that there are spiritual ministry gifts also set in the church for the spiritual needs of the body. And with all of these, there is the necessary unction of the Holy Ghost to complement each function, and empower them to the fulfillment of God's purpose and design.

In a small church, all this gets somewhat foggy, but as the church grows, the need for plurality of elders becomes more apparent. In a smaller traditional church the "one pastor," along with his spiritual ministry function, is usually required to pay the bills, answer the phone, prepare the bulletin, visit the sick and function as a secretary, janitor, maintenance man, etc. We know all too well that in the beginning of a new church, nearly every function becomes the responsibility of that "one pastor". However, as the church begins to grow, transition of responsibilities needs to be made as soon as possible. Otherwise, the ministry becomes tradition, and no one grows into their calling. It is clear that only the Holy Ghost can lead us properly into these areas.

This traditional scenario is played out thousands of times across the board in most churches. Most new churches try to be "like the other churches" around them or like the churches in their specific sect or denomination. Even very small churches have "pastors". They are like Israel, when they wanted a visible king to rule over them instead of God. The reason was that they wanted to be "like the other nations." God's plan was better. He would rule through the voice of the prophet, as we see in Jeremiah chapter seven. But it wasn't the way the other nations did it. And Israel wanted to conform to the traditions of the land.

God's plan for the church is clear and is confirmed by many scriptures concerning Elders. The details of how that all works may not be fully clear to us yet. But perhaps God is calling us to make some changes in our churches, bringing them more in line with scriptural example.

Understanding Plurality

A major problem is that there is not a good understanding or recognition in the church at large of the scriptural principle of Elders. While this whole system of "plurality" may seem confusing, we clearly see in scripture that there is a plurality of "ministries" set in the church. Without trying to identify certain functions by name we will just speak about the "minister".

Many of the same identifying marks that determine if the minister is effective are applicable to most ministries. By ministries we mean apostles, prophets, evangelists, pastors, teachers, miracles, healings, helps, administrations, diverse tongues, elders and deacons. This most surely is not an all-inclusive list.

The ministry is set in the church to be effective, and not just to fill a position because one is vacant. It is often assumed that all who are called of God are automatically equipped to be "ministers". Simple experience will tell us that this is not true.

Paul said not to appoint a new convert. Sometimes it is difficult to make a distinction in maturity between a new convert and an old convert. Effectiveness must be learned. Preaching should be, ideally, by the anointing, but the day-to-day diversity of ministry surely must be learned. If we assume that by "ministry," we mean leadership, administration, decision-making, and overseeing operations, we are implying that an organizational performance is the function. Thus, effectiveness is the goal.

Since a poor or confused leader is no leader at all, it should be clear that an ineffective ministry couldn't be classified as "leadership". The corporate function of overseeing the church must be the necessary hierarchy.

In this time period, the church has come under all kinds of liability and lawsuits against its ministries and members. A small mistake can result in millions of dollars in damages. If one member strikes another member while on church property, the church is automatically involved. If a "minister" gives counsel that proves to be wrong, both the minister and the church may be charged. Therefore, correctness *and* effectiveness must be the goal of each person of the corporate ministry.

This effectiveness can be learned, and a system of average methods of handling routine situations can be implemented for the "ministry". While effectiveness of ministry can be learned, it cannot be taught as a class-room subject. This is one of the things that must be taught by God.

It is written in the prophets, 'And they shall all be taught of God.' Everyone who has heard and learned from the Father, comes to Me. John 6:45 (NASB)

If there is no intimacy with God, how will God teach? This is a big problem for diverse ministries. This fact makes church leadership very different from corporate leadership.

Effectiveness in ministry must begin with self-discipline. A "minister" who has no self-discipline cannot be a leader. They might pray for the sick and do a general service in the church, but one who has no discipline in his/her life cannot be a leader and an example to the flock. For example; a leader who consistently shows up for the meeting half an hour late disqualifies him/herself from leadership, because s/he is not an example to the church. S/he may well have a calling, but is ineffective because of the lack of self-discipline. His knowledge or her gift will not substitute for the lack of discipline as far as leadership in the church is concerned. One may pray for the sick and they may get healed, but that is not the same thing as leadership.

Discipline is the foundation of competent ministry, and competent ministry adds to the person's spiritual life, growth and development. Spiritual development adds to the organizational development, which adds to the corporate effectiveness.

For the most part, we have only considered the effectiveness of a minister, and have not evaluated the church by any measure of corporate effectiveness. If we believe that Ephesians 4:11 is valid today, then corporate effectiveness is the accurate measuring rod for the church. Corporate effectiveness is the result of corporate ministry.

The Apostle Peter shows us the process of corporate effectiveness in participating in the Kingdom of God.

Shepherd the flock of God among you, exercising oversight not under compulsion, but voluntarily, according to {the will of} God; and not for sordid gain, but with eagerness; nor yet as lording it over those allotted to your charge, but proving to be examples to the flock. 1 Peter 5:2-3 (NASB)

The congregation's perceptions of the minister will either contribute to his/her effectiveness and the reception of the word s/he speaks, or it will utterly negate it. That bears repeating: A negative perception of a minister will negate the word s/he speaks. What the minister says may be true, but it lacks validity because of the perception of the minister.

A minister who is always begging for money is perceived as having no faith. If a minister with an anger problem preaches on the peace of God, his word is not believable. He is not an example of the word he preaches. If a minister who is always looking lecherously at members of the congregation preaches on morality, his/her word is not believable. If a person whose mind is in the gutter preaches about setting your mind on things above, such words fall to the ground. A super-carnal minister looks ridiculous preaching about spiritual life!

Many assume that anyone who preaches from the scriptures will be effective because "God watches over His word to perform it" and "the word will not return to God without accomplishing what God sent it for". However, the minister must present a consistent life of discipline to make his words effective, acceptable and believable, or they will just fall at his/her feet. Everything is not just by the "mystery" of the anointing as some say. That anointing must flow through the life of the minister to the people. This was the secret of the effectiveness of the Apostolic church. Since the people receive the word through the minister, if they reject the minister, they reject the word of the minister.

It is most common these days for a minister to have both a spiritual and an administrative function in the church. That is, s/he both preaches or teaches and also administrates the church. This requires the minister to vacillate between the inspirational and the conceptual, the mechanical and the procedural, from revelation and intuition, to answering the phone and paying bills, from the burden of the word, to the responsibility of counseling and overseeing the mechanics of the church. This is quite disruptive and probably impossible, but this situation was also faced in the early church.

But select from among you, brethren, seven men of good reputation, full of the Spirit and of wisdom, whom we may put in charge of this task. But we will devote ourselves to prayer, and to the ministry of the word. Acts 6:3-4 (NASB)

The first church understood the necessity of separating these responsibilities. It seems evident that the minister must focus on what his/her particular contribution to the church should be. A minister does this by determining his/her calling, grace, anointing, and place of greatest effectiveness. If s/he thinks he can "wait on tables" and still be effective in the word and in prayer, then s/he is better equipped that the apostles were!

If a minister is ineffective in his/her calling, then s/he is probably ineffective in waiting on tables also. If a minister cannot discipline him/herself enough to think through and discover his/her effectiveness, s/he will remain ineffective. Such a minister will quit, break down or have to be transferred. And then, the cycle begins all over again.

Common Mistakes

One common mistake of "the minister" is to set goals for the church without setting goals for his/her own life and ministry. For example: S/he may project a plan to have 1000 in Sunday school in two years, but have no plan for his/her own growth, inspiration and leadership. An influx of people will demand much more organizational planning for "the minister" and for the corporate ministry.

It should be obvious that 1000 more in church meetings will require much more discipline on everybody's part. The minister's individual goals should integrate into the organizational goal of the church. If not, there could be a tremendous conflict between the two.

Another common error is preaching a progression of scriptural information as the basis of church ministry without focusing upon developing Christian character, insight, foresight, vision, faith, courage, hope, dedication, determination, consecration, inspiration and discipline in the congregation. (One author has encountered people who were raised in the Apostolic church, over the age of 40, who could quote Acts 2:38 and could prove the Oneness of God, but did not comprehend the difference between telling the truth and lying. They had learned only doctrine, but had never grown spiritually in their entire lives. True doctrine without true Christian character is pointless. The pharisees also understood true doctrine, but never learned anything more about living for God.)

Having 200 people with informational knowledge is not the same thing as having 200 people with Christian virtue, in other words, 200 people with the foundation for Christian ministry and leadership!

A huge problem in many churches is the sin of jealousy: If "the pastor" (in the traditional church model) feels threatened by "young leaders" rising up and being recognized and sought after by the congregation, his/her ministry will become ineffective because s/he has deviated from the scriptural principle:

And the things which you have heard from me in the presence of many witnesses, these entrust to faithful men, who will be able to teach others also. 2 Timothy 2:2 (NASB)

If "the pastor's" aim is to raise up spiritual men and women as leaders so s/he can leave and continue his/her ministry, then that must be his/her personal goal. New leaders aren't a threat to the "ministry," but the fulfillment of the ministry. The "new leaders" may not be a testimony of brilliance and genius, but if they have seriously chosen to serve God, "the pastor" will teach them the same as s/he was taught and prepared.

A true story demonstrates what can happen when a minister's own jealousy and insecurity, not to mention ego, are threatened as God raises up other ministers. This situation took place in an Apostolic church some thirty years ago. Following a prophecy given in the church concerning a major change that would bring great revival to the area, the following events happened: The pastor took on a co-pastor, a well-known Apostolic evangelist. The previous assistant pastor was leaving to open a new church in another city. The incoming minister, owing to his name and reputation, was named co-pastor rather than assistant.

Prior to their departure, the assistant pastor and his wife had been witnessing to their neighbor lady, a divorced Catholic woman with four children ranging from four to thirteen. This lady consistently refused to visit the church, maintaining that she was a Catholic. Upon learning that her neighbors were moving away, she reluctantly agreed to visit the church. That Sunday morning, she and her three oldest children received the Holy Ghost and were baptized in Jesus' name. She brought with her the same stubbornness with which she had resisted coming to church, and channeled it into her zeal for the things of God she was just beginning to learn.

Three weeks later, this Sister marched into the office of the elderly pastor, and informed him that God had told her to take over the youth group. Now, we all know that new converts, being zealous, can sometimes get confused. Sometimes they think God has told them something that He really hasn't. And this lady was so new, she didn't even really know the doctrine yet. But the real reason the pastor was so sure she was mistaken was because the church didn't have a youth group! There was a very small handful of teenagers, mostly backslidden. They might pray through once a year at youth camp, but more often than not, they spent service outside the church smoking.

But this dear Sister would not be dissuaded: She dismissed the pastor's facts as irrelevant. God had shown her a vision of 60 teenagers living for God and evangelizing the area! The pastor couldn't talk her out of it, so he relented, and gave her charge of the teenagers. Six months later, the church had a powerful youth group, scores of young people, on fire for God. Their leader would take them out to parts of the county outside the city, and they would evangelize. And a harvest began to be realized. The church began to grow, and there was a tremendous feeling of revival and rebirth in the air. That area of the country, one of the last mission fields of the Apostolic church, was on fire.

And then, the trouble started. Satan won't allow God's work to proceed unchallenged. And he will look for the weakest link. In this case, it wasn't the youth group leader, or any of the teens; it was the new co-pastor. This man, fond of boasting about how many souls would be in heaven because of him, became insanely jealous of the admiration the youth group leader received for the work she was doing. He began working to sabotage it. Without going into the ugly details, the result of it all was that the church polarized, and then split apart. The move of God came to a screeching halt. Before all was said and done, this co-pastor had even tried to talk one member of the youth group into suicide, and when that failed, tried to blackmail him. For more than thirty years afterward, there wasn't even an Apostolic church within the city limits there, and many, if not most, of the former youth group members are no longer living for God. All this, because one man thought himself more important than the ministry God was raising up. We can only dream about what might have been if that move of God had been allowed to continue. And out of all of it, that same minister was allowed to continue on in a new church he founded after the split, and then to return to the evangelistic trail, receiving praise and accolades everywhere for his great ministry. This is NOT what God intended for His church and His ministers!

Preparation for ministry involves two aspects of learning. One is to acquire scriptural knowledge, skill in the word of God, good work habits, and personal discipline. The other has to be to un-learn the many things that are not relevant to Christian ministry.

Mixing secular psychology, as well as many other secular things, with Christian ministry is a corruption that pollutes the purity of ministry. Of course, no minister is totally free from those things, but we should all be aware: We need to un-learn those things.

On the other hand, much of ministry is just a rational decision made out of an informed and renewed mind. Everything is not super-spiritual and inspired. Ministry is a co-operation between God and man. There are certain things that are clearly spoken of in the scriptures, and therefore do not require prayer and fasting. For example: If someone is contemplating marrying an unbeliever, we don't need to pray and fast for guidance. While no one begins as an expert, at least some of ministry is just rational and sound judgment based upon scripture. Being able to minister rational facts without offending is a learned skill.

Ministry Lifestyle

The ministry is not a path that is clearly marked out and it is definitely not meticulously labeled for us to follow. We still need to be led by the cloud, the same as Israel. Therefore, unless we walk with God, we will find ourselves completely over our heads and lost in the desert of confusion.

Simply put, ministry has to do with "calling," while the minister's life has to do with "practical living." The minister must soon learn there is so much more than the "calling" and grace and the anointing. All of those things deal mostly with our effectiveness to others. The "lifestyle" has to do with knowing God and developing an intimate relationship with Him.

The "calling" will soon get confused and foggy unless the "lifestyle" is primary. There is "the calling," "the one who is called," and "the One who called." Without this perspective, the calling will deteriorate into activity instead of personal development and maturity. Activities can be accomplished in the flesh, but the lifestyle and the intimate relationship can only be attained by spiritual development.

In the early church, the ministry was entrusted to common people who achieved tremendous and uncommon performance in a brand new field of ministry that didn't draw upon decades of past experience. Today, we have nearly 2000 years of history and hundreds of books written about the ministry. Still, we all have to begin without much experience. For many of us, experience is gained by making mistakes. We might assume that the early church ministry was inspired and supernatural, while ours is more learned. However, when we see the problems the early church faced and the errors they made, we see that very little has changed. Problems, like the personality conflict between Paul and John Mark, still have to be sorted out. And often, they are not. The Bible is not a complete manual on what to do and what to say in every single situation that comes up.

Not all ministry is logical and rational, but neither is it irrational. It may seem naturally illogical, and yet be spiritually logical at the same time. It is logical by inspiration, and not by rational thought.

Administration is much more logical. We don't need to pray and fast to find out if we should pay the bills. A good testimony *demands* that we pay the bills. Administration is more mechanical, but every bit as necessary as spiritual ministry. That being said, it is far better to have a spiritual person doing mechanical things than a carnal person. And a carnal person doing spiritual things will always be a disaster.

The minister should be in a state of continuous growth. The minister who never tries to improve his/her ministry is doomed to mediocrity and insignificance. If s/he sees no reason to improve his/her message or effectiveness or insight into the scriptures or clarity of his/her vision, s/he condemns himself to mediocrity. There needs to be a continual desire to improve the meetings and the praise and the worship and the ministry of the word.

Participation in the assembly should be the ongoing goal for each member, or boredom and monotony will soon set in. It seems evident that when things become routine, momentum stops and growth stagnates. One author recalls visiting a small Apostolic church in the southwest about 40 years ago. Every service was exactly the same, with exactly the same people in attendance. No one seemed to have any desire to see the church grow. No evangelism was done, and their baptismal tank had been empty for many years, because there was nobody new to baptize. They had great music, and knew how to shout. But they were stuck in a rut, bored, and just going through the motions.

The minister should be advancing personally, spiritually and intellectually as the church continues to develop. Old goals should be reached and new goals set. There should be new challenges and new God-given directions.

The children of Israel coming out of Egypt are a clear example of this: Joshua, leading Israel into conquering the promised land, is a clear example of new challenges, advancing in a new direction, and attaining new goals. A moving church attracts new people with new calling and new zeal. The advancing atmosphere of the church motivates faith and expectation, and most importantly, action.

Ordinary people can be motivated to a higher level of consecration and to higher performance by a motivated and consecrated ministry. (Remember the youth group leader mentioned in the previous chapter.) Unfortunately the opposite is also true: A dead ministry promotes death.

A word of warning, all this forward motion and activity must take place in the setting of godly and moral standards and a righteous life. A fast-moving, immoral minister is speeding in the wrong direction. Spiritual advancement can only be built and motivated by the strong message of the Kingdom of God, and God's personal government in each life.

The divine laws of eternity in personal experience are the foundation of spiritual development and the advancement of the minister's personal walk with God. A busy minister who has no idea of what the will of God is will be full of activity, but doing nothing. Nothing can be accomplished by legalism or routine busyness in the life of the ministers. Only moral and spiritual development produces effectiveness in the assembly. An effective minister will be seen in the testimony of the church in the society around them: A spiritually healthy church will be a viable and visible force in the community.

Visitors can sense boredom in the minister even if they are not born again. A minister in frustration and boredom is a minister in despair, and is not a force within or without the church. On the other hand, visitors can sense life and excitement. It is a great mistake for the ministry to teach people how to act like they have life and excitement in order to attract new people!

The minister will not be able to be used by God to meet the needs of the church until his/her own needs are being met. Individual function and fulfillment of the minister is necessary before s/he can be effective in the church. The responsibility of the ministry is not to give ministers a function, but to inspire them to seek God for a function.

The problem of individual boredom will not go away simply by attracting new members, but only by the individual functioning in a specific calling, doing the will of God. New members sometimes seem to contribute to the frustration of old believers, especially if the new members quickly find their place and begin to function. Thus, the ministry must encourage even old-time saints to find their position in the body, and to function in it.

Therefore, the organizational goals for growth must be in tandem with the individual member's requirement to be equipped for ministry, and motivated to achieve a satisfactory usefulness in the body of Christ. Adding more unequipped and useless members only serves to create an endless array of problems.

It perhaps requires a ministerial juggling act to balance the organizational needs for growth and development with the individual and personal needs of growth and development of the members. The primary need is for the individual believer to be trained and equipped to take their place in the body of Christ. They need to be inspired to seek God for that place and opportunity, and to work for the organizational growth and development. In other words: The organizational growth and development will depend upon the individual being equipped to minister when the organizational growth takes place.

To put all our effort into organizational growth before there is multilevel help prepared is a common error of evangelically motivated churches. The entire ministry is focused on increasing numbers, while the equipping of the saints is neglected. The equipping of the Saints to do the work of ministry MUST be primary.

The equipped member must find his/her function and effectiveness in ministry in order to achieve contentment and satisfaction. Without it, s/he will not feel like a member of the body of Christ. Just "taking it by faith" is too shallow. It can be achieved only by functioning in a meaningful ministry, and not by doctrine and more information. Without a ministry, without a function, boredom sets in. The "ministry" becomes ineffective. The "trainees" must be taught to listen and make effective use of what is ministered, so that they, in turn, can become effective ministers.

It's important to realize that the main purpose of Sunday service is training and equipping the saints to do the work of ministry. Sadly, it doesn't often happen there. However, we don't set any other time for it, either. The result is that it doesn't happen, and we have a church full of "people" and a minister or two on the platform, instead of a congregation of ministers, each with their own vital function in the body. We need to think of the Christian church as a Christian school: it is a place for teaching and training. While in school the tests and grades determine the effectiveness of the effort, the results of the ministry may not be that immediate, and sometimes it may take years to see any fruit from the effort. Nevertheless, if the saints are properly equipped for ministry, and each is fulfilling their role, the church will function as God intended.

What is going on in the hearts and minds of the trainees for the ministry is a great mystery. It is possible that only 1 in 100 (or even 1000) will respond even though all are called to the service of the King. Either the ministry is ineffective or the hearers are hardening their heart. (If the minister is effective in delivering the message of the Kingdom, but the hearers harden their hearts and refuse to respond, the minister will still receive his reward. Jeremiah was faithful when he was sent and delivered the correct message even though no one listened. In that case, the fault was with the hearers.)

While we have no direct power over the hearts of others, we do have the power to make the ministry effective, and that must be our goal.

Reality Check

It would seem from our study of scripture that it would be ideal for a church of 200 to have 200 people "ministering". Obviously, it is not possible for 200 to preach, but it is possible for 200 to be involved in various aspects of church ministry. However, we should ask ourselves if that is how it will be in our present day reality.

Can we even imagine the problems that would arise for the Elders with 200 people trying to "minister"? In the world's largest church (in Korea), there are thousands who minister. The problems must be tremendous, but the results are obviously effective, since the church is still growing.

We all have the tendency to reject various solutions because of the perceived problems. It is easy to be so overwhelmed by the fear of new problems, that we don't seek God or receive revelation from His Word. If we let ourselves be crippled by fear, we will never accomplish anything for the Kingdom.

It is possible for numbers to grow while a congregation remains static. There will always be subtle attacks upon the church, and the leadership must be alert to changes in the assembly. A multitude of day-to-day problems could be caused by demonic attacks, and the changes that take place are the result. The Elders must not become so busy "handling difficulties" that they are unaware of the disasters that may have an irreversible impact upon many souls.

One limitation upon the "leadership" of a church is that they are primarily functioning within the organization and their contribution is seen primarily in the field of instruction. What the people do with what they have been taught is entirely up to them. They may hear anointed teaching about loving their neighbor, but then go and fight with their neighbor.

The ministry does not have direct control over the lives of those in the church. Those ministers who have sought to change that by trying to control the lives of the members have had to revert back to some form of legalism. Legalism will always remove the grace from their lives.

I am the vine, you are the branches; he who abides in Me, and I in him, he bears much fruit; for apart from Me you can do nothing. John 15:5 (NASB)

This verse signals the universal incompetence of man, whether a minister or a new believer. If this fact is not recognized, we develop a false hope that with us, or with our believers, it will be different. As the branch cannot bear fruit without the vine, so no ministry can produce anything eternal without everything flowing out of Jesus Christ.

"Nothing" in this verse does not mean that we cannot build a large congregation and create a diversity of activities. Therefore, it must mean that without the centrality of Christ in our meetings, we can produce nothing *eternal*. We can build with wood, hay and straw by ourselves and out of our own cleverness. However, wood, hay and straw are not eternal. Every minister who would be effective will acknowledge his/her universal incompetence.

The C.E.O. type of minister who tries one idea after another, beginning a new program after the last one failed, condemns him/herself to ineffectiveness. Those people who are impressed with activity will never recognize this as total failure, but will instead believe that the next idea will be a success. Most ministries consider effectiveness as being abstract, while God views effectiveness as only that which flows out of Himself.

The environment within the assembly is the ministry's responsibility. Outside the assembly, and in the home, must be the member's responsibility. However, most members view their environment as abstract, because most of the time they have no control over the atmosphere in which they work. This cannot be the situation in the worship service, or with the atmosphere in which the word of God is presented. The environment is critical to the effectiveness of ministry. It is the inside of the church that is most visible to the "pastors" and is the realm of their work.

However, the organization of the church should also be an effective agent to the society outside the assembly. The effort and fulfillment of the church as a power is seen in its function outside, in a hostile environment.

Members of various minorities are faced with discrimination and intolerance on the outside daily. Society is always exaggerating and overstating the difference between the races, etc. The church must be a sanctuary where there is no distinction between the races, because race is totally irrelevant in Christ. The same goes for gender distinctions, financial distinctions and distinctions in sexual orientation. In Christ, none of these things matter. We are all created equal and are formed together in one body! In the church everyone is equal and everyone is a vital member. This spiritual atmosphere is the ministry's responsibility.

A carnal atmosphere is not conducive to spiritual training. An effective performance in ministry outweighs areas of weakness of the minister. However, performance does not outweigh character and morality. An immoral minister will always be ineffective. Everyone has limitations and weaknesses, but they don't hinder our areas of God-given strength. Weakness doesn't cancel out strength, just as darkness doesn't cancel out light.

If a foot cannot think, it doesn't destroy its unique effectiveness as a foot. If the foot is eliminated because it cannot think, the whole body is crippled. The foot must be evaluated against the task it is designed to do, and not on whether it can do everything! While all men are fallible, every necessary job in the body can be done by somebody. The impossible job is not for men, but for God.

A doctor or a psychiatrist searches for weakness and tries to treat it to make the person strong. Their first concern is to identify weakness. In the physical body this seems normal. In the body of Christ this is not profitable. The primary question should be: what can this member do? We should look for potential, and not weakness. We all have weaknesses, but if we magnify or focus on them, we accent the failure that is bound to result.

If Jesus had evaluated Peter by his failure, Peter would have been eliminated. But Jesus saw that the immediate need was that Peter's faith not fail. Strengthening his faith was more important than focusing on the failure.

Searching for the strength of each member is much more profitable than focusing upon the weakness. Function inspires more function, and identifies the strength... if the function is according to grace. Function in the flesh just manifests more flesh. Some who never find their function are just carried along by the organization. The organization becomes a substitute for function.

God does not promote on the basis of seniority, but on the basis of faithfulness in small things. All who are born again, i.e., baptized in Jesus' name and filled with the Holy Ghost, have the potential to be effective members. Potential and effectiveness, however, are two very different things. Sometimes effectiveness may be a matter of opportunity, but more often, it is a matter of faithfulness in the small things.

Faithfulness will find/create the opportunity. The faithful worker will look for any opportunity to work, and thus, will be effective. Some years back, some members of a congregation in Puerto Rico were complaining because the Pastor wouldn't let them work. It is true that their pastor didn't assign them work to do. And the reason he didn't was because it

didn't appear that they really *wanted* to work.

Some churches seem to progress by assigning every member a task to do even if it is ushering once a month, working with the children or greeting at door. We should expect more from the members of the body of Christ.

It is assumed by many that "the pastor" is a manager of people. Many pastors who cannot adequately manage themselves set out to manage others. After many years in business and in the church, we doubt it can be proven that a "manager" can actually manage people. A person who only works when you are present will not be an effective worker when you leave. A sloppy worker in the work place will most likely be a sloppy worker in the church. A good worker will be a self-starter and will continue until the job is complete. "The management" should not have to stand over a worker to assign each phase of the work or to make sure the work was done. People in the workplace know that, but the people in the church must still learn that.

Effectiveness can and must be learned. Even a self-starter who wants to work still has to learn to be an effective worker. No one is born a pastor or an elder or a minister. God must give grace, the Holy Ghost must anoint, but the ministry is still learned.

Our commission is to make disciples of every nation, teaching them. Is it possible that we will each be evaluated by how effective we were in making disciples? Not so much on how many came to the meetings, or how well we preached, but did we actually make disciples?

The size of the organization is not important because we only have close contact with a few of the total. It is difficult to have a close relationship with more than 12 people even if we have 2000 in the meetings. Each of us has an immediate circle of associates, and we are effective with those we contact regularly. However, the church evaluates us by our effectiveness in the corporate whole. When that responsibility is placed upon one man or woman who is called "pastor", s/he will surely fail. Even if "the pastor" is expected to disciple just 100 persons, s/he will be limited to teaching general things that apply to the whole group, and will not be able to individually teach each one who may qualify as a disciple. Corporate presidents know that, but the church still has to learn that.

Even though our understanding of scriptural truth and the word of God may be very good, our effectiveness in making disciples among the nations has been very poor. Busyness should not be confused with effectiveness: One who appears to just plod along in the eyes of others may in truth be the most effective. Very few are "naturals" at making disciples.

Their effectiveness will be directly related to their guidance and being taught by the Spirit of God.

There always seems to be a shortage of workers. The laborers are always too few for the harvest. Therefore, we have a tendency to accept any who are willing to work without worrying too much about their ability or their effectiveness. No corporation would accept leaders that way. Even though in industry and in business there are thousands upon thousands who are effective, the church seems to have difficulty preparing effective ministry.

While there is no shortage of schools to teach the basics of doctrine, sermon preparation, church history, etc., there is serious deficit in other areas. Such schools, and the organizations that utilize them, rarely take into account a student's calling or abilities. Instead, they rely on tradition: Men who graduate are expected to evangelize for a year or two. Then they either become a (super) pastor, or they stagnate on the platform in a church with another (super) pastor. It matters not if they are called as Apostles, and should be opening a new church, or as Teachers, or Prophets. They are told by the church and tradition what to do, instead of by the one God who called them to be ministers in the first place.

For a woman, the situation may even be worse: Her calling and gifts may be completely ignored, and she will be relegated to teaching Sunday School, playing the piano or organ, or leading the choir. While some Apostolic churches will allow her to be licensed, even those won't always recognize her as a minister. (Forty years ago, in one of the largest Apostolic organizations in the US, a particular district had one female minister. She had a local license, but ordination was not available to her. This was an elderly woman, a pioneer of Apostolic Pentecost, but because of her sex, she was not allowed to reach her full potential. And to add insult to injury, the District Superintendent would not acknowledge her as a minister. She was not invited to the meetings of the other ministers in the district.)

By following these traditions. the Apostolic church has effectively crippled itself. By forcing men to become Evangelists or Pastors, they deprive the church of Apostles, Prophets and Teachers. And they instead supply the church with Evangelists and Pastors who may not have any gift or grace for those ministries. And by refusing women access to the ministry, they effectively diminish the potential leadership by more than half. And make no mistake, this is tradition, NOT scripture. It is too easy and convenient to take Paul's remarks about women out of context, and to use it as an excuse to restrict our Sisters' access to ministry. But women were part of Jesus' ministry from the beginning, going from city to city with Him, and supporting Him with their own money. Women were active in the early church. Mary, the mother of John Mark, and Lydia were Pastors, and Lydia may well have been the first Bishop in Philippi. Priscilla was an Evangelist. (The fact that her name was written before her husband's on at least one occasion tells us that she was the primary preacher. In that century, a woman's name never preceded her husband's unless she were more important in some way, for example, wealthy, noble, etc. Priscilla and Aquila were tent makers, so she was neither wealthy nor noble. Therefore, it seems evident that she was the lead evangelist on the team.)

It is essential for the church to put away the traditions that have crippled our leadership, because without the Apostles, Prophets, Evangelists, Pastors and Teachers, there will be no one to equip the Saints for ministry. And since there is neither male nor female, nor Jew nor Greek (and by extension, neither black nor white nor any other fleshly consideration) in Christ, it is essential that ANY Saint of God be free to hear and respond to the specific call God has given, and not be forced into a predefined role by the church. God calls men and women as it suits Him, and only He should determine what ministry they will do.

Afterword

It is the hope of the writers that the material that has been presented here will assist the men and women of God who are called to work for the Kingdom of God.

Following the Apostolic example laid down in the New Testament is the way to ensure that our churches function and grow like the first century church. The traditions handed down from the Protestant Reformation may have served us for a while, but they are imperfect, having been designed by men. God has a better plan, and it behooves us to abandon our old traditions for the even older pattern that He Himself established for His church. In everything, we should strive to be fully Apostolic, earnestly contending for the faith once delivered to the Saints. If this does not extend beyond matters of doctrine, then we have failed to be the Apostolic church.

About the authors

Nathaniel Morales began ministering the Gospel of Jesus Christ since he was 18 years old. He grew up in a strong Pentecostal home where every-one was active in ministry. His parents were both preachers who pio-neered several churches throughout the Eastern seaboard of the United States.

Over the next 30 years, Brother Morales has served as a Teacher, Mis-sionary, Associate Pastor and Senior Pastor. He has been actively in-volved in planting and pastoring churches in the United States as well as in Puerto Rico and Mexico, with a passion to help train and raise up new leaders to take their place in service and ministry to the whole body of Christ.

Pastor Morales well understood the needs of the local church. His de-sire has always been to help bring a clear and balanced word to that local church until all come to the unity of the faith and are built up into the fullness that God wants for all of His people to experience.

William H. Carey was born in Brooklyn, and grew up there and in Galway, NY. He was filled with the Holy Ghost in 1972, and baptized in Jesus' name six months later. His ministerial and theological training took place at the Apostolic Pentecostal Bible School and the Wide World of Truth Ministries Bible School, both formerly in Schenectady, NY. Bro. Carey began studying Greek at the age of 12, and Hebrew at the age of 19, and has studied many other languages, including Russian, French, Italian and Irish.

The former Pastor of Living Springs Apostolic Church in Omaha, NE and Lighthouse Apostolic Church in Schenectady, he has helped train new ministers since the early 1980's. Bro. Carey is the author of the curriculum used in the Apostolic Institute of Ministry, the ministerial training school of the Affirming Pentecostal Church, Inc., and serves as Director of Apostolic Education for that organization. He resides in Ferndale, MI.

www.ingramcontent.com/pod-product-compliance
Lightning Source LLC
Chambersburg PA
CBHW082106140626
46553CB00018B/1097